DAVID GOTTLIEB

is a sociologist and Professor of Human
Development at The Pennsylvania State
University. He was Director of Research for
the 1970–1971 White House Conference on
Children and Youth, and has published many
articles and books on "coming of age" in
America, including *America's Other Youth:
Growing Up Poor.*

CHILDREN'S LIBERATION

Edited by David Gottlieb

A SPECTRUM BOOK

PRENTICE-HALL, INC., ENGLEWOOD CLIFFS, NEW JERSEY

Library of Congress Cataloging in Publication Data

GOTTLIEB, DAVID.   comp.
  Children's liberation.

  (A Spectrum Book)
  Includes bibliographical references.
  1. Children in the United States.   2. Youth—
United States.   I. Title.
HQ792.U5G68   301.43'1'0973   73–4036
ISBN 0–13–130831–9
ISBN 0–13–130823–8 (pbk)

© 1973 by PRENTICE-HALL, INC.
Englewood Cliffs, New Jersey.

A SPECTRUM BOOK

10 9 8 7 6 5 4 3 2 1

Printed in the United States of America

PRENTICE-HALL INTERNATIONAL, INC. (*London*)
PRENTICE-HALL OF AUSTRALIA PTY., LTD. (*Sydney*)
PRENTICE-HALL OF CANADA, LTD. (*Toronto*)
PRENTICE-HALL OF INDIA PRIVATE LIMITED (*New Delhi*)
PRENTICE-HALL OF JAPAN, INC. (*Tokyo*)

This anthology is dedicated
to five beautiful and,
hopefully, liberated children:
Amy
Peter
Michael
Rebecca
Sara

CONTENTS

Part Two: Perspectives

ACKNOWLEDGEMENTS

First, my thanks to those authors who have allowed their work to be included in this anthology. Others have, of course, contributed to the concept, development, and preparation of this book.

My gratitude for patience, insight, and cooperation of two colleagues must be declared. To Ms Virginia Sibbison for her careful reading of the manuscript, for her keen eye in noticing errors—be they in concept or grammar. To Ms Anne Heinsohn for her efficient handling of manuscript logistics and review of the manuscript.

To Ms Karen Herhold for her willingness to read, edit, type and retype, and still come back for more.

My gratitude is also extended to my good friend Thomas J. Cottle. In many ways the special love and understanding felt and expressed by Tom Cottle were stimuli for the undertaking of this project. To Tom, then, my continued friendship and deepest respect.

To Michael Hunter of Prentice-Hall my thanks for your encouragement and cooperation.

INTRODUCTION

The major purposes of this book can be stated simply and directly. The first is to make clear that despite a national reluctance to believe otherwise, American children are in too many instances victims of indifference, intimidation, abuse, exploitation, and vengeance. The second is to identify the many areas in which there are flagrant contradictions between the warm, loving, and concerned rhetoric of adults (be they parents, teachers, judges, social workers, congressmen, or presidents) and the manner in which they actually deal with children.

The primary motivation for this book is not to take advantage of the current social climate, which seems to encourage publications and documentaries dealing with the plight of the poor, of minority groups, of women, and of the aged. For in reality, no matter what one's education or political ideology there is some degree of consensus that these groups have indeed suffered and been discriminated against. In the matter of children this is not the case. On the contrary, so great is the conviction that children are the chosen people of our nation that we are more than reluctant even to explore the possibility that our treatment of children is lacking in love, compassion, decency, or respect.

That we love our children is assumed. We are reminded again and again through the mass media, the declarations of political leaders, the commentary of parents and professionals—and even through the multitude of commercials encouraging us to do for our children—that we not only have an obligation to our children but that this obligation flows from our love for our children. How many times has each of us said (most often in an exchange with a child who has fallen short of our expectations or desires) "It is for you that I work hard"; "It is for your future that we have sacrificed"; "It is for your good."

When we are shown hard evidence of child abuse and exploitation our reactions are mixed with some horror and much disbelief. Our response is that these are rare and deviant cases. We so firmly believe in our love for our children that we view those who inflict pain upon children as sick and bizarre. What we fail to recognize is that what we do hear and see represents only the tip of an iceberg. There is much, much more. As we will attempt to point out in the essays and discussion that follow, the variety of child abuses is great and not limited to a few isolated settings. We will also seek to make clear that although the children of poverty and the children of minority groups may suffer most, few children are spared. In essence, then, the major goal of these collected essays is to shake us out of our cultural lethargy, to begin to bridge the gap between what we think, what we feel, what we say, and what we actually do with our children.

There is no single adult audience, no special-interest or professional group for which these essays are meant. This is not a "how to do it" book for parents or teachers. It is, hopefully, a book that contains something of interest and value to all adults, for in reality every adult plays a critical role in the life of a child.

The essays included in this book were written by people of very different backgrounds and interests. Among the authors are a sociologist, an economist, and a lawyer. The areas they cover include economics, education, health, families, leisure time, laws, the administration of justice, health, and the social and physical environments of our nation. In addition, the essays reflect an eclectic methodological approach. Some pieces are based upon quantitative data and empirical inquiry. Others flow from the experiences of people who have worked with and dealt with children in a variety of settings. Still others are based upon historical analysis. And finally some combine the three methodologies and reflect the efforts of scholars and laymen. This variety of viewpoints and methods is deliberate, indicating that our concern is not with any one group of children. As there is more than one American, there is more than one American child. Children are not a monolith, and there is no social institution that does not play some part in what happens to them. Hence our concern is with all children and all societal agencies and institutions.

This is an impassioned book, deliberately aimed at exposing and describing the many ways in which American children are victimized. Each author, no matter what his background or methodology, has as a primary concern the welfare, dignity, and freedom of children. But despite these strong feelings, the book is intended as a fair and accurate assessment of children in the United States.

The opening essay, "Children in America: A Demographic Profile and Commentary," provides data dealing with who the children are, where they live, how they live, their health, their families, their homes, and their communities. In addition, this essay points out the relationships between a child's family background and his present status and future life chances.

The next essay, "Children as Victims," focuses more specifically upon the many ways and the many settings in which American children become victims—victims of those who seek political power, victims of those who seek control, victims of those who seek release from their own frustrations, victims of those who seek to perpetuate their own professional and personal ideologies. The material in this essay illustrates how even "well-meaning" adults can become so entangled in their own needs and desires that they lose sight of their expressed purpose—to improve the condition of children. The gap between the way we talk about children and what we ultimately do to them is demonstrated by the behavior of concerned adults—concerned adults at the 1970 White House Conference on Children, concerned adults involved in the issue of school decentralization, concerned adults responsible for planning and implementing educational programs, concerned adults responsible for the child-centered mass media, concerned adults involved in assessing and explaining variations in the intelligence and performance of children. Finally this essay shows how, win or lose, the child remains the victim. If the child succeeds in fulfilling adult expectations, the praise is given and the status awarded to the adults involved. If the child fails, he takes the blame. Efforts are made to modify his behavior. Rarely are serious efforts directed toward modifying the behavior of the adults and the adult-controlled institutions that contribute so significantly to the frustration of children.

The next essay, "The Exploitation of the American Growing Class," deals with the economic structure of American society and the impact of industrialization and urbanization on families and children. Numerous examples are cited to illustrate that our actual economic investments in the health, education, and welfare of our children belies our expressed concern for the young. The author also makes the point that where we do provide necessary care our motivation is not solely altruistic or primarily a result of our wish to see our children free and happy. Instead, all too often our basic concern appears to be the generating of a future human resource that will guarantee the continuation of our current social and economic systems.

"Children and the Justice Process: Reality and Rhetoric," the fourth essay, is a historical and social analysis of the forces that led to the emergence of the juvenile court and children's prisons. The author's observations and analysis indicate that in the case of legal rights children might have fared better had they been spared the efforts of well-intentioned adults. Evidence is presented that makes it apparent that being a child may well increase the probabilities of unfair, unconstitutional, and inhumane treatment.

The four essays so far discussed serve as an introduction and backdrop to those that follow. These remaining essays are not out of a common cloth. The first, "The Emergence of Identity," is one of the reports presented to the delegates of the 1970 White House Conference on Children. The authors consider the concept of identity and the critical importance to children of the formation of a positive and meaningful identity. Particularly important is the discussion that shows the many ways and the many areas in which "the emergence of a healthy sense of identity is damaged by continuous failure and by situations in which the child senses that he is less than others." The report concludes with a number of programmatic and policy recommendations.

An essay by Thomas J. Cottle, entitled "Parent and Child—The Hazards of Equality," deals with the old but still important theme of young people's involvement with adult authority. In this essay the author describes both the fragile quality of child-adult relationships and the conflict experienced by the young in their dealings with adult authority—a conflict in part between the child's need and desire for independence and his need and desire for adult support and, in some instances, adult control. Cottle provides case-study vignettes to show the ways in which the upsetting of the delicate balance between the generations can prove disastrous for both child and adult.

The essay by Paul Lerman, "Delinquents Without Crime," is based upon an analysis of data dealing with young people who have been labeled delinquents. The data and commentary provided by Lerman are both illuminating and frightening. Illuminating in that his discussion reveals information about the young and the criminal-justice system of which few are aware. For example, Lerman points out that "juveniles are subject to stricter laws than adults, and to more severe penalties for noncriminal acts than are many adults who commit felonies." The frightening dimension of the Lerman essay is that even where there is knowledge and awareness of the inequities and cruelties of the system little corrective action is taken.

The essays by Norman K. Denzin, "Children and Their Care-takers," and George B. Leonard, "How School Stunts Your Child," deal with children and schools. In light of the fact that more and more children are spending more and more time in school, both articles take on added importance. Both articles lend credence to a growing feeling that many schools invest more time, expense, and energy in the control of children than in providing opportunities for learning and healthy social development. Both authors note the ways in which our schools, not unlike other social institutions, force the child into the role of victim: victim of rules and regulations, tired and frustrated teachers, and expectations and academic standards over which he has little if any control. That some children will rebel, that some will break under the pressure, and that most will silently surrender should not be surprising.

The final selection, also one of the reports of the 1970 White House Conference on Children, deals with the social environment in which children are reared. The authors begin with the following observation:

> The children of America are the future of America, yet they are now far from being the nation's first priority. Both public policies

and programs and our actions as individuals shape a world in many ways inhospitable, indeed often hostile, to the life of children and their full creative growth.

They go on to point out the ways in which the physical and social environments are connected and how both in combination distort the life chances of children. Although the evidence presented in this report makes clear that it is poor children who will suffer most, it is also apparent that no child can escape the harmful elements of our physical and social environments. This report, like others presented at the Conference, concludes with a series of recommendations.

Part One: Overview

CHILDREN IN AMERICA: A DEMOGRAPHIC PROFILE AND COMMENTARY

David Gottlieb

Although American children are confronted by similar social institutions and similar social problems, it is not reasonable to believe that they represent a monolith. As there is more than one American, there is more than one American child.

There are the children of poverty, the children of affluence, the children of factory workers, policemen, and bus drivers, and the thousands of children without fathers. There are black, Chicano, Puerto Rican, and Indian children; children of a multitude of ethnic, racial, and religious backgrounds; children of farms, villages, suburbs, cities, and reservations. There are too many children who are institutionalized, children who are sick—physically and emotionally. There are too many children abandoned or abused by those who are supposed to care for them.

7

HOW MANY CHILDREN

According to the Bureau of the Census, of a total American population of over 205 million in 1970, some 54 million, or over one-fourth, are children fourteen years of age or younger. Almost half (47 percent) of all Americans are under twenty-five years of age. Although whites continue to be the vast majority in our country (88 per cent in 1970), the nonwhite percentage has increased from 10 percent in 1940 to 12 percent in 1970.

WHERE THEY LIVE

Over 70 percent of the U.S. population now live in urban areas. Over 60 percent of the children under fourteen live in metropolitan areas; less than 5 percent of all children live on farms.

Since 1950 the combined migration patterns of different racial groups have led to a situation in which the urban areas contain a higher percentage of blacks than whites. Interestingly the rate of urbanization in the past few decades has been greatest for American Indians. Nevertheless, 400,000 Indians continue to live on reservations.

THEIR ECONOMIC CONDITION

The Economic Report of the President in 1970 stated, "America enters the 1970's a wealthy nation, which is growing wealthier at a rapid rate." Despite this encouraging observation it is apparent that many needs remain unmet. Economic, educational, social, and health benefits are not distributed equally. In 1970, of the 48 million children between the ages of six and seventeen, 7 million were reported to be living in poverty, as were 3 million children out of 23 million under the age of six.

It should be kept in mind that the poverty statistics cited above are relatively low, given the rising cost of living and growing unemployment. Ten million children out of 71 million existing in poverty is a shocking and frightening report, but it is a conservative estimate—in reality the figure is greater.

Although nonwhites represent only 12 percent of our total population, their children comprise 40 percent of all children in poverty. Federal government reports show a decline over the past ten years in the proportion of poverty families; nevertheless, these same reports make clear that it is nonwhites who are least likely to benefit from national prosperity. Even with equal opportunity legislation, nonwhites continue to fall further behind in their attempts to catch up with whites. Black fathers, although their educational status may be the same as white fathers, hold lower-level jobs and earn lower wages.

THE WAY THEY LIVE

As there is more than one type of American child, there is more than one type of American family. In the essay, "The Exploitation of the American Growing Class," we will deal in greater detail with the varying structure and dimensions of American *families*. For our immediate purposes it will be sufficient to mention only two facets of child concerns. In 1970 7 million children under the age of fourteen were being raised in families from which the father was absent. Here as in the distribution of other resources, we find significant differences between whites and nonwhites. In this case, nonwhite children are three times as likely as white children to be raised in fatherless settings.

Although more professionals are now being trained and there has been an increase in service-related agencies, possibly no more than half the children in need of aid (economic, social, educational, psychological) are receiving help from child-welfare agencies. As of 1969 it is estimated that some 250,000 children were living in foster homes and another 75,000 in institutions.

THEIR HEALTH

As a result of preventive health measures and a reluctant recognition of the realities of the situation, the incidence of many diseases associated with childhood has generally declined. However, some diseases remain widespread and the incidence of others has increased. Again, it is important to point out the conservative nature of available statistics. These statistics represent what is known—that is, what is reported. It is generally recognized that many children are afflicted with any one of a number of diseases that remain undetected, undeclared, and hence unreported. It is also recognized that incidence of syphilis, gonorrhea, hepatitis, and drug addiction has increased and continues to increase, particularly among children and young people. It is important to note that just as positive benefits are not distributed equally, neither are detrimental and negative attributes. Poor and nonwhite children are most likely to be afflicted and least likely to have access to corrective and rehabilitative resources.

The health status of children in the U.S. cannot be estimated solely by the presentation of incidences of disease. We know that accidents remain a major threat to a child's health. Some 15,000 children under the age of fifteen die from accidents each year. Another 19 million children are injured severely enough to seek medical care or to restrict their usual activity. Emotional and mental illness continue as major child health problems. Reported estimates only disclose a limited part of a much larger phenomenon. In 1968 it was estimated that 682,000 children under the age of eighteen were receiving some type of assistance with problems designated as emotional.

According to the National Institute of Mental Health:

- An estimated 5 percent of children needing psychiatric care are receiving it.
- In 1968 approximately 10 percent of the 50 million school-age children had moderate to severe emotional problems.
- One out of three poor children had serious emotional problems that required attention.

In other health related areas as well the picture is generally far from encouraging. Available data provided by the U.S. Public Health Service indicate that:

- One out of twelve children had a speech defect (1963–1965; ages six–eleven).
- One out of nine children had defective vision (1963–1965; ages six–eleven).

• One out of four children had never seen a dentist (1963–1965; ages five–fourteen).

There are, in addition—and in this case even approximate estimates are difficult to come by—thousands of children who are physically abused and beaten by adults. The deliberate physical abuse of infants and children is in fact so pervasive in our society that many see it as the major health problem confronting our children today. Obviously a child who is a victim of physical abuse suffers emotional and mental anguish. Although few empirical inquiries have dealt with the familial and social factors associated with infant and child abuse, there is some evidence that this type of behavior is not unique to any single economic or ethnic group. The available data suggest, however, that the assumption that the adults most likely to attack children physically are the poor and uneducated is indeed a false one. Rather it would appear that in many instances the poor are the most protective and loving of their young, regardless of the dire circumstances in which they find themselves.[1]

It is also apparent that the abused child is frequently a child who was not wanted by his parents. Despite the wider distribution of birth control devices and a changing attitude toward birth control, many unwanted infants are born. Estimates provided by the U.S. Department of Health, Education and Welfare indicate that nearly 60 percent of married women (between the ages of eighteen–forty-four) report more pregnancies than wanted, or pregnancies earlier than wanted.

The demographic data so far presented provide a general profile of American children. The remaining portions of this essay deal with data that are unique to specific developmental stages of a child's life.

THE PRENATAL PERIOD AND INFANCY

The prenatal period is clearly a critical stage. A child's destiny is shaped in part before birth. The physical and mental health of the expectant mother has a major influence upon the present and future well-being of the infant. The mother's physical and emotional condi-

[1] Leontine Young, *Wednesday's Children* (New York: McGraw-Hill Book Company, 1971).

tion, in turn, is influenced by such factors as age, marital status, socio-economic status, race, and the availability of assistance resources.

The impact of race emerges once again in dramatic fashion when comparisons are made between white and nonwhite infant mortality rates. While infant mortality rates (defined as the number of deaths under one year of age per 1,000 births) have declined, the rate is almost twice as high for nonwhites as for whites (19.2 for whites, 34.5 for nonwhites). International comparisons show that the United States has a higher infant mortality rate than Japan, France, Norway, Denmark, the United Kingdom, and East Germany.

Race is also related to the chances of a mother surviving the birth of her child. According to data provided by the U.S. Department of Health, Education and Welfare, the maternal mortality rate (defined as the number of mother deaths per 100,000 live births) was, as of 1967, more than three times greater for nonwhite mothers than for white mothers (69.5 versus 19.5).

Reliable statistics dealing with abortions are, as might be anticipated, difficult to obtain. Obviously many women are reluctant to admit to induced abortions, hence available estimates must be considered extremely tenuous and conservative. Data provided by the 1970 White House Conference on Children note that in 1967 some 830,000 illegal abortions were performed in the United States. The combination of liberalized abortion laws and greater acceptance of birth control devices should reduce both the proportion of unwanted children and the number of abortions performed by unlicensed and unqualified practitioners. At the same time, however, it is important to point out that birth control devices, knowledge of such devices, and opportunities for utilization of legalized abortion services are not equally distributed among all segments of the population. Economics, education, and age are factors associated with the availability and utilization of such services. The data dealing with patterns of illegitimate births suggest that it is in fact the young and the poor who are most in need of assistance in matters of birth control information and services. Comparative data indicate that between the years 1940 and 1968 there has been a steady increase in the number of illegitimate live births. These same data make clear that it is among the poor and the young (mothers between the ages of fifteen and nineteen) that illegitimate births are most likely to occur. It is also apparent that the young and the poor, who will confront the greatest difficulty in their attempts to rear a child, will also encounter the greatest resistance in their efforts to obtain necessary counseling and services.

Between 100,000 and 200,000 of the babies born each year are considered to be mentally retarded. The causes of mental retardation can be identified in approximately one-fourth of the cases. This one-fourth is usually linked to genetic abnormalities, infections such as German measles during early pregnancy, birth accidents, postnatal infections, or trauma. In the remaining cases, the vast majority, the factors responsible for retardation are not considered to be exclusively physiological. Rather they are factors that can frequently be anticipated and prevented. Other factors believed to be causes of mental retardation include inadequacies in prenatal and perinatal health care, nutrition, child rearing, and social and environmental opportunities. In other words, with an appropriate investment of resources it would be possible to reduce significantly the number of babies who come to be identified as mentally retarded.

There is also growing evidence that many children labeled as mentally retarded could have, with adequate assistance, been spared institutionalization. Given a less rigid view of what is normal, acceptable, or appropriate behavior, fewer children would be designated as "retarded" or "abnormal." Given a reluctance toward "institutionalization" and an endorsement of policies of family and community based intervention and assistance, many children would not have to be insulated from their families and communities. Unfortunately, as in other cases of perceived "deviant" or "abnormal" behavior, our approach has been to isolate the individual. Too often, under the pretext of doing what is best for the sick or injured child and his family, we remove the child from those settings that offer the love and individual attention the child most needs.

Examples of this pattern of societal rejection and child abandonment are numerous. Our traditional approach has been to treat the child as if he, rather than the society or some yet to be discovered factor, is responsible for his condition and our discomfort.

THE PRE-SCHOOL YEARS

From the ages of one to six the child is increasingly exposed to, and influenced by, sources outside the home. While home life continues to play the major role in his socialization, the child becomes more dependent upon the social institutions and conditions of his neighborhood, community, and society.

For many young children, exposure to formal socialization by adults other than parents begins before enrollment in kindergarten. Increasingly large numbers of pre-school children are entering nursery schools and other types of child-care facility. During the five-year period between 1965 and 1970, the number of children participating in nursery school or day-care arrangements more than doubled (from half a million in 1965 to over a million children in 1970). The greatest growth in pre-school enrollment has occurred among nonwhite lower-income families. The motivating factor for such enrollment is not necessarily a commitment to the belief that such an experience is best for the young child. Rather, for many parents, particularly the poor, these arrangements provide a setting where children can be housed so the mother will be free to work. Similarly the enrollment of middle-class children in pre-school programs cannot be viewed solely as reflecting a primary concern with the development of the child. Many parents do tire of their children, and nursery school does provide one means for adult escape.

More important, perhaps, the increased enrollment in pre-school programs as well as the prolonging of formal education contribute to further fragmentation of the family and a growing dependency upon others to train and rear one's children. The prolonging of the child's socialization and relegation of this responsibility for socialization to individuals outside the family are frequently not in the best interests of the child. It is worth pointing out that despite our constant verbal support of family closeness we continue to develop mechanisms that separate parents from children and generation from generation.

The segregation of parents and children, whether voluntary or by necessity, has increased dramatically during the past century. Not only do children spend more time in school than ever before, but they are also encouraged to become involved in their own age-segregated, leisure-time pursuits. The increase in child segregation appears to be correlated with an increase in adult desires for independence, mobility, and individual fulfillment. Clearly there are parents who do not choose to be separated from their children. But it is also clear that many parents, in a desire to achieve their own self-fulfillment, relegate the needs and interests of their children to a secondary level of concern.

During the past two decades employment has become increasingly prevalent among mothers of school and pre-school children. In 1969 more than half the mothers of children between the ages of six and seventeen were in the labor force. There were nearly 12 million working mothers with children under eighteen in 1969. Although most of these working mothers were from families with relatively low incomes, many were not employed out of economic necessity.

The question being raised here is not whether mothers should or should not work. It is not our intent to deny the importance and value of adult fulfillment. Nor are we saying that there are not legitimate reasons for removing some children from homes in which they are ignored or abused. Rather we want to point out the marked discrepancy between our child-related, expressed attitudes and our behavior. We stress the need for intensifying family association and cohesion, yet we do not utilize pre-school care as a beneficial, supplemental agent to the needs of both parents and children; rather we attach the stigma of pathology and financial hardship to it. As a consequence, we grudgingly tolerate the growth of various types of pre-school facilities but do nothing to insure that their programs enrich the experiences of the child and fit the expectations and preferences of the parents.

As always, we claim to have the best interests of the child in mind when we push for the enrollment of the child into any sort of program that will release his mother for work or leisure. The available empirical evidence, however, suggests that there are several critical variables that must be considered in the placement of a child in a pre-school program. These variables are unique to the individual child in some cases (for instance, age, physical health, degree of security and self-sufficiency) and specific to the program in others (is there adequate stimulation of all types? are the staff members warm and loving? does the center or nursery school provide nutritious food? and so on). It is indeed unfortunate that most pre-school programs up until this time either have been custodial in nature (particularly those of the lower class) or have concentrated on "teaching children to play together" rather than on dealing with the very real potentials of young children for growth and learning.

The following statement from a report of the 1970 White House Conference on Children would certainly suggest that there is a real need to take a more critical look at the impact that existing pre-school settings may have upon children:

We know very little of the quality of care given by non-maternal sources in the home, but of the outside arrangements, far too many are unlicensed, unsupervised and chosen because they are the only available care alternative. Even the many dedicated women who put effort and love into their "family care" or nursery school lack the training and the educational, medical, physical and financial resources to meet the needs of a growing child. A recent nationwide survey of child care has turned up far too many horrifying examples of children neglected and endangered in both licensed and unlicensed centers.

Obviously pre-school programs are not the only institutional settings of potential harm to our children. In other sections of this book we will deal with how schools, laws, the economic system, and families contribute to the abuse and exploitation of our children.

In his opening remarks to the 1969 White House Conference on Foods, Nutrition and Health, President Nixon stated:

> A child ill-fed is dulled in curiosity, lower in stamina, distracted from learning. The cost of medical care for diet-related illness; remedial education required to overcome diet-related slowness in school; institutionalization and loss of full productive potential; all of these place a heavy economic burden on society as a whole.

Although the President's emphasis on the eventual national economic consequences of early childhood malnutrition represents a cold and detached interpretation, it is an accurate statement. It also represents an honest approach, since the President recognizes that more humanistic and emotional arguments do not necessarily generate the funds and policies needed to resolve the problems of child hunger. Rather it is the cold argument of cost-benefit ratios that will have the higher probability of generating legislative action.

Data provided by the U.S. Department of Health, Education and Welfare for 1968–1969 show that the diets of pre-school children often lack adequate amounts of important nutrients. These same data indicate that more than half of the children under the age of six in this country receive inadequate supplements of vitamin A, many do not receive sufficient riboflavin, and others lack vitamin C and iron. Comparisons of relationships between family income, race, and adequacy of diet show an all-too-familiar and expected pattern: the poorer you are, the poorer your diet. What these data do not communicate is the fact that the richest nation in the world has failed to stop the hunger and malnutrition of millions of its citizens. Despite an endless series of national conferences, TV documentaries, and legislative hearings, thousands of American children do not come close to receiving even the bare minimum of an adequate diet.

SCHOOL YEARS

The major element in the socialization of American children has become the school. Statistical reports make clear that more and more children are attending school for longer and longer periods of time. While the debate about the quality, structure, substance, and dignity of the educational process continues, we still insist that our children acquire as many educational credentials as possible. What our schools do to many of our children and the overall consequences of the prolonging of this "educational training" process will be dealt with in another section of this book. Here our concern is with the more quantifiable aspects of children and American schools.

As of 1969 ninety-nine out of every one hundred children between the ages of seven and thirteen were enrolled in some type of school. At each age level, a higher percentage of white children than of nonwhite children was enrolled in our schools. The discrepancy between the races becomes most pronounced at the high school and university levels. Historically, at virtually every educational level a higher percentage of whites than of nonwhites, of affluent than of poor and working-class children has been enrolled in American schools. Only during the past twenty years have significant efforts been made to open our educational institutions to all children. Still, a marked discrepancy continues to exist in both educational opportunities and the quality of education provided. The poor and the nonwhite find our schools, not unlike other institutions in our society, unresponsive.

In many communities the emigration of the middle class has led to a decline in state and federal concern with educational quality and a decline in educational funding. The result is that hundreds of thousands of children in need of counseling and education find themselves in schools lacking the resources critical to a relevant and sound developmental program. Although there is verbal recognition that those children who come from families in which parents have had minimal formal education are most in need of compensatory and supplementary help, little of this assistance is provided. For example, we know that a large majority of black elementary school pupils are from homes in which the family head is not a high school graduate. In fact, in the United States in 1969 black elementary school children were twice as likely as white elementary school children to come from families where the family head had completed fewer than twelve years of formal education.

Inability to read effectively is a major educational problem. One out of every seven elementary school children has a reading problem. At the same time, according to the U.S. Department of Education, the problem is most prevalent among school children of low-income families. More than one in five low-income children has a serious reading disability.

The tendency has been to abandon the notion that educational deficiencies can be remedied by the school. There is an increasing tendency to feel that no matter what efforts are made by the school, certain children (particularly the less affluent and nonwhite) are incapable of normative educational achievement and behavior. Shifting the burden of proof from the school to the child becomes a convenient strategy for not dealing with the obvious inadequacies and injustices of our educational practices and policies. The available evidence, however, supports the observation that feelings of dissatisfaction with our schools and failure in educational achievement are not limited to the poor or minority groups. Student alienation and underachievement have become very much visible characteristics among white middle-class children. Data dealing with modal grade performance (the grade levels usually associated with age) indicate that while the proportion of black children below their modal grades is greater than that of white children, the proportion of black children above their modal grades is also higher than that of white children (U.S. Department of Commerce, Bureau of Census, 1969).

The growing discontent with our schools among the middle class is reflected in the emergence of the new school and free school movements. These educational innovations represent a countereducational approach. Unfortunately the majority of Americans cannot afford the costs of private schools. In addition, the geographical location and style of such new and private schools prohibit attendance, even though nonwhites may be capable of paying the costs. Comparisons of whites and nonwhites of similar incomes show that at each income level more whites than nonwhites have children who are enrolled in private schools.

Again, the point must be made that while all children may suffer from certain inadequacies and indifferences of our social institutions, alternative remedial and rehabilitative opportunities are not equally distributed. In the case of our schools, general discontent has resulted in the stimulation of new organizational structures and procedures for a select elite and the abandonment of serious efforts to change the structure and procedures of those schools that deal with the vast majority of our children.

One manifestation of the failure of our schools and of our society to deal adequately and reasonably with our children is the growing incidence of juvenile delinquency. Even though acts of juvenile delinquency are frequently age-based offenses (that is, if these same offenses were committed by adults they would not be classified as criminal or illegal behavior), there has been a marked increase in the incidence of delinquent behavior and a trend toward more serious and costly offenses.

According to data provided by the U.S. Department of Justice, about one fifth of all individuals arrested in this country in 1969 were under sixteen years of age. Twenty-two percent of all individuals arrested for crimes of violence were under the age of eighteen. Fifty-four percent of all those arrested for property crimes were under the age of eighteen. Over 60,000 children (under the age of fourteen) were arrested for being runaways; 13,000 children (ten years old and younger) were arrested for vandalism; 16,000 children (under the age of twelve) were arrested for disorderly conduct. Recognizing that these are reported crimes and do not include those of juvenile delinquents who were neither apprehended nor reported, the overall picture is one that calls for more than repeated demands of "law and order." There are more visible signs of both the law and structural order in our schools today than at any other period in American history. Policemen are on duty on a regular basis in many elementary and secondary schools. In numerous communities law enforcement officials can enter schools, interrogate students, and conduct searches of students and their possessions without prior warning or warrants.

More and more law enforcement officials have been assigned to "Youth Divisions." Modern technology has been utilized increasingly in efforts to identify and apprehend youthful offenders. The greater surveillance and control have not, however, brought about a decline in delinquency, nor have they led to the development of more effective preventive and rehabilitative strategies. On the contrary, our current approach seems to have generated greater generational polarization, more fear and anxiety, higher rates of arrest, and an increase in the number of younger children placed in correctional institutions. If progress in resolving juvenile delinquency is to be measured by arrests, then we have been successful indeed.

In 1956 twenty out of every one thousand children between the ages of ten and seventeen came before a juvenile court in the United States. By 1968 the proportion increased to twenty-nine out of every one thousand children in this age group. According to projections published by the U.S. Justice Department, we may anticipate, unless changes occur, that one out of every nine American children will appear before a juvenile court before he reaches his eighteenth birthday.

SUMMARY AND CONCLUSIONS

The presentation of demographic data dealing with the current status of American children was clearly not the sole purpose of this essay. Statistical data, even when portraying the conditions of the poor, the abused, the illiterate, and the frightened, cannot do justice to those who are in fact poor, abused, illiterate, or frightened.

Still, statistical data are of value since they provide us with a more systematic and accurate accounting of who the children are and what the status is of their childhood. From such a presentation we should be better able to recognize that, despite our technology, our affluence, our expertise, and our rhetoric, children from every part of the country, children from every socioeconomic background, children of every race, religious, and ethnic group, *do* experience and endure some pain, some abuse, and some humiliation as they go about the business of growing up in America.

Statistical presentations serve yet another purpose. In a society that encourages rational and systematic reasoning, in a society that is uncomfortable with spontaneous displays of emotion, in a society that worships technology and endorses the scientific approach, "hard data" will frequently receive greater attention than will the more dramatic and humane message.

Hard economic arguments and promises of enhanced social control are more likely to generate social change than are pleas for the freedom and dignity of man. In part, the greater responsiveness to hard, cold logic reflects a growing American exhaustion with discussions and presentations of our social problems. The prevailing social climate is one in which people appear to have been so battered with horror stories of war, poverty, racism, conflict, and man's general inhumanity to his fellow man that they now desperately seek escape. The mood is one of privatism, of turning inward—a social phenomenon in which individuals either seek to discount the seriousness and magnitude of problems or take the position that the individual, not the social structure, is at fault.

Hopefully the combination of hard data and interpretive commentary will stimulate discussion among those who have the power and resources to enhance the growth and development of our children. Clearly these data indicate that no child can fully escape the harmful workings of our social system. It is also clear that none of us, regardless of his current age, status, color, sex, or role, can fully isolate himself from his children and his society.

CHILDREN AS VICTIMS

===

David Gottlieb

As we begin this significant national reassessment, let us remind ourselves of our purpose.

This should be a Conference about love . . . about our need to love those to whom we have given birth . . . and those who are most helpless and in need . . . and those who give us a reason for being . . . and those who are most precious for themselves—for what they are and what they can become. Our children.

Let us ask what we want for our children. Then let us ask not less for all children.

We want for our children a home of love and understanding and encouragement.

We want for our children a full opportunity for learning in an environment in which they can reach and grow and take pride in themselves.

We want for our children the right to be healthy, to be free of sickness. But if sickness comes, to have the best care humanly possible.

We want for our children the right to have the respect of others.

23

We want them to have respect and dignity as a *right* because they are, not because of who their parents are.

We want for our children to live under laws that are fair and just and that are administered fairly and justly.

We want for our children to love their country because their country has earned their love, because their country strives to create peace and to create the conditions of a humane and healthy society for all of its citizens and is dedicating the resources necessary to redeem its commitment to these ends.

This we want for our children. Therefore this we must want for *all* children. There can be no exceptions.

To those who have food, it is intolerable that there is a child somewhere in our land who is ill-nourished. To those who live beneath a sound roof, it is intolerable that there should be a child who is ill-housed and without adequate clothes.

That we are well, so then is it intolerable that a child is needlessly sick or lives in an environment that poisons his body or mind.

That we have the knowledge, so then is it intolerable that there is some child who does not have a full opportunity to learn.

That we are a Nation founded on equality, so must we not tolerate intolerance in ourselves or our fellows.

We must recognize that there is some child in special need. And he especially must be our child.

At a time when it is all too easy to accuse, to blame, to fault, let us gather in trust and faith to put before the Nation that which is necessary and best. All this we say with the greatest sense of urgency and conviction.

Our children and our families are in deep trouble. A society that neglects its children and fears its youth cannot care about its future. Surely this is the way to national disaster.

Our society has the capacity to care and the resources to act. Act we must.

There is a need to change our patterns of living so that once again we will bring adults back into the lives of children and children back into the lives of adults.

The changes must come at all levels of society—in business, industry, mass media, schools, government, communities, neighborhoods, and, above all, in ourselves. The changes must come *now*.

We as Delegates to the 1970 White House Conference on Children do now affirm our *total commitment* to help bring our Nation into a new age of caring. Now we begin.[1]

---

[1] *Report to the President: White House Conference on Children* (Washington, D.C.: U.S. Government Printing Office, 1970), p. 5.

This moving statement was the preamble presented to the assembled delegates of the 1970 White House Conference on Children. Unfortunately, as is so often the case, there soon emerged a marked discrepancy between the words expressed in defense of children and the behavior exhibited by those adults who had unanimously endorsed a *"total commitment* to help bring our Nation into a new age of caring."

The self-serving desires and goals of different adult professional, ethnic, racial, and political groups contributed to an atmosphere of confrontation, dissent, and dysfunctionality. Having agreed to the need for a renewed crusade for children, the assembled adults then struggled to determine just who should lead the children's crusade. The end result consisted of hundreds of recommendations, numerous minority reports, and something in writing for each and every adult group and organization attending the conference. No professional, social, ethnic, racial, or political group was denied. Advocates of education, of social welfare, of local, state, and federal government, and of day care did their thing. Each group made certain that the final report of the conference included a recommendation that would help perpetuate its particular ideology, profession, or approach. Recommendations were made for the establishment of numerous "National Institutes"—an institute for everyone: an institute for the study of the family, the study of health, the study of education, the study of welfare, the study of environment, and the study of judicial processes.

Although the majority of delegates had agreed that past approaches and existing institutions were inadequate, there was little motivation to eliminate or restructure these arrangements as part of a comprehensive effort. And although most delegates expressed the opinion that we had overfragmentized child-centered services and were now competing for meager resources, few of them were willing to abandon their approach, their profession, their organization, and their demands for more funds in order to facilitate a more unified, wholistic approach to the needs of children.

It is not surprising then that by the time the conference was concluded most participants felt it had been a hollow exercise. Few thought that the deliberations or recommendations would lead to societal changes in the treatment of children. It is significant to note that few delegates held themselves or their particular constituency responsible for the conference's failure to achieve its expressed goals;

the failure of the conference almost invariably was attributed to some other group or to some other individual. The admission of failure is not a characteristic of professionals. Blame was placed upon others through such comments as "it was the minority group people," "it's the establishment," "it's the system," "it's the old timers," "it's the young radicals," or "it was poor organization."

Two years later the prophecy of doubt and failure has been fulfilled. Nothing really has changed. The adult delegates have returned home and continue to function in the same manner and in the same institutional settings as in the past. The children continue to be dealt with as in the past. The children remain the victims.

The events and outcomes of the 1970 White House Conference on Children do not represent a freak or unique occurrence. On the contrary, there is abundant evidence to support the proposition that adults speak with hypocrisy. Again and again adult rhetoric rings with concern for our children even as adult behavior reflects indifference toward and exploitation of our children.

Various examples of the dichotomy between adult words of concern for the child and adult behavior patterns of indifference toward children are presented in the following pages. We begin with Martin Mayer's analysis of the teacher-community confrontation in the now famous Ocean Hill, New York, struggle over school decentralization. Following an in-depth review of the history of the confrontation, Mayer concludes with the following observations:

> But there were no real issues in the strikes—just slogans. What is ultimately disgusting about the teacher strikes and the public officials who failed to prevent them is that words like "community control" mean no more in dealing with the complex of relationships between school administrators and parents than words like "quality education" mean in dealing with the inadequate teacher training and severe multiple deprivations which combine to produce so much wretched work in our slum schools. On words like these, people who knew better created a confrontation.
>
> During the course of the crisis, a member of the Mayor's Urban Task Force told a meeting of architects that he thought the strikes would do good by showing people how important education is. One can, perhaps, be a little more precise about the impact of the teachers' strikes. They accelerated the flight from the city's schools—and indeed from the city itself—of those who can afford to leave. They made companies which had thought of establishing themselves in New York decide to shun the city. They poisoned the wells of

human decency which did exist in this cosmopolitan and sophisticated metropolis, which the mayor only three years ago called "Fun
City." And they will very probably reduce to the condition of Boston
and Alabama, or some mixture of the two, a school system which
was wretchedly ill-organized and weakly led but relatively alert
intellectually and by no means so completely ineffective as it has
become fashionable to say—and which was almost the only hope
the city could offer for the future of hundreds of thousands of
Negro and Puerto Rican children.[2]

In reviewing the public rhetoric surrounding the Ocean Hill conflict, one can only be impressed with the continuous concern expressed
on behalf of the children. Each group emphatically denied that it was
an issue of its own power or self-determination and sought to make
clear that its behavior was guided by the single goal of providing
children with the education and training that would enable them to
become productive, healthy, and dignified citizens. Each of the parties
—teachers, administrators, and parents—waved the child-loving banner. Each questioned the sincerity and integrity of the others, no
matter how similar the declared goals. Ultimately, as Mayer points
out, the issue was no longer what was best for the children. Instead
the issue became one of fulfilling the needs of adults, even if these
needs were not of direct benefit to the children.

The events of Ocean Hill do not represent an isolated or single
case. Again and again we are able to note how children are used as
pawns in the political and social arena.

Some twenty years after the Supreme Court decision about
school desegregation, the President of the United States declared a
moratorium on school-busing. Once again the stated intent was to
protect the children from tedious travel and to enhance their educational growth. The welfare of "all the children" was the President's
rallying cry. But even the most naive of citizens recognized that the
primary motivation for the busing moratorium was political.

In each case, whether the issue be education, employment, welfare, health, or bussing, it is apparent that children are without power.
It is equally apparent that children have little control over or influence with the social institutions that shape their lives. Yet somehow
they must manage to live with the consequences of the acions of those

[2] Martin Mayer, "The Full and Sometimes Very Surprising Story of Ocean
Hill, the Teachers' Union and the Teachers' Strike of 1968," *The New York
Times Magazine*, February 2, 1969, p. 71.

who do have that power and control in our social institutions. If adults in our highly complex and impersonal society feel a sense of power-lessness and a lack of control over their destinies, it does not take much in the way of imagination to appreciate how removed and how insignificant children must feel.

Of course many would reject the argument that our children are exploited or treated with indifference. The counterargument is that our children are better off today than at any time in our history. After all, they have more toys, more recreation, more education, more "fun" than we ever did as children. If the quality of life for individuals is to be measured solely by material accumulation, then many of our children do have it made. If, on the other hand, the quality of one's life is to be measured by such factors as freedom of choice; control over one's educational future and environment; equal rights without regard to age, sex, race, and economic status; and access to alterna-tive life styles—then our children are probably far worse off than in years past. For in reality our children are being increasingly segregated by age, race, sex, and socioeconomic status; blocked from pursuing alternative educational and socializing settings; isolated from the de-cision-makers, whether in the home, school, community, or nation; insulated from the world of work and career exploration; and denied the opportunity to be listened to and taken seriously.

Whereas in the past our children were at least respected for their potential as economic contributors to the family, this is less and less the case today. Instead our children have become increasingly dependent upon us—economically, psychologically, and socially. The combination of extended economic investment in our children and the prolonging of their "adult preparation" contributes to the belief that it is our duty and right to control every aspect of the child's life.

Since children are seen as extensions of their parents, and since they are increasingly dependent upon their parents, they carry a double burden. As Bettelheim points out:

> All this is only part of the attitude that expects American children to do better than their parents, and often, seen objectively, the task is even quite feasible; but to children and adolescents the demand seems emotionally impossible, because it comes at a time when their opinion of their parents' achievement is unrealistically high. Con-trary to all psychoanalytic writings that teach clearly how the child

and adolescent is over-awed by his parents' power and wisdom, both society and his parents continue to expect the emotionally impossible of youth.[3]

Children are placed in a position in which they are victims of a social system over which they have little control or influence. In most cases society has arbitrarily assigned goals that children are expected to achieve. The means by which these goals are to be achieved are equally arbitrarily defined. Norms of appropriate behavior, dress and language have also been established. The child is expected to act, think, feel, and believe in a prescribed manner. The established ground rules for expected behavior do not always represent what the child needs or desires. Nor do the ground rules frequently take into consideration the fact that many children, because of societal conditions, cannot possibly achieve expected goals, although they may be the very goals that they seek to pursue. The combination of arbitrary societal ground rules, social institutions that pay only lip service to the needs and conditions of the young, and a lack of the child's involvement in decisions affecting his life can only lead to increased child failure, alienation, and emotional crippling. However, when the child does fail we do not examine the role played by the social system and its institutions. Rather, when the child fails to conform (that is, fails to behave in a manner deemed appropriate) he is considered deviant—he is the problem. Having classified the child as deviant, underachieving, or delinquent, we turn to strategies of individual rehabilitation and behavior modification.

Rarely do we implement strategies of institutional rehabilitation and modification. Rarely will we go beyond the making of statements about cold and indifferent bureaucracies and unfeeling and indifferent teachers, parents, social workers, and policemen. Despite the evidence that the failure of our children often flows from the inadequacies and injustices of our social institutions, we blame the child. Despite our awareness of the shortcomings of our child-rearing practices and policies, we continue to focus upon changing the child rather than the very institutions and laws that have created our "problem children."

The technique is one of blaming the victim. William Ryan, in

[3] Bruno Bettelheim, "The Problem of Generations," in *The Challenge of Youth*, ed. Erik H. Erikson (New York: Anchor Books, 1965), p. 84.

his excellent book *Blaming the Victim,* illustrates how this technique operates when explanations are offered to account for the inability of poor children to compete with more affluent children:

> This is the folklore of cultural deprivation as it is used in an ideological fashion to preserve the care of the status-quo in urban education—to forestall any questioning about the fundamental problems of recruiting and training teachers, achieving racial integration, and, in particular, governing the school system. Waving this banner, educationists can advocate Head Start, smaller classes, more effective schools, "scatteration" to the suburbs by one-way busing, teaching machines, or Swahili—almost anything that involves changing or manipulating the child. They fight to the death any proposal that implies there might be anything at all wrong with the teacher or the teaching, and resist any exploration of, or intrusion into, the monopolistic control of public education by the teaching profession, particularly if it implies participation in decision making by laymen from the community.[4]

The child as powerless victim of adult needs and exploitation may also be noted in an examination of the mass media provided for the young. Clearly children do not control or directly influence the form and content of the media to which they are exposed. They are not the writers, producers, directors, or publishers. Whether it be periodicals, books, television, radio, movies, or recordings, they are the consumers. Given the quality of the various types of mass media directed at them, they are in reality victims both of innocuous and irrelevant content and in many instances of exploitative and false advertisement.

According to the Report of the 1970 White House Conference on Children:

> Mass media have an overwhelming influence on the lives of our children and, consequently, the future of our society. Television, particularly, plays a dominant role; through grade school, children spend more time in front of their television sets than in front of school teachers.[5]

An awareness of the impact of television upon children has not generated much in the way of worthwhile programing for children. With

[4] William Ryan, *Blaming the Victim* (New York: Pantheon Books, 1971), pp. 34–35.
[5] *White House Conference on Children,* p. 325.

the exception of token programs that are considered to be of some merit, the profit motive continues to be the salient factor.

The reluctance and indifference of those who control the media to change the content and focus of both programs and commercials directed at children are well documented. According to a report published in 1954 by the National Commission on the Causes and Prevention of Violence, television industry spokesmen took the position that the research evidence concerning the effect upon children of violent portrayals was inconclusive. Still, they did acknowledge that there was a possible risk of adverse effects, and for that reason the industry had adopted standards and regulations to govern the portrayal of violence. The television authorities made two promises: first, to conduct systematic research in order to determine the relationship between viewing violence and exhibiting violent behavior; second, to reduce the amount of violence on television.

The report of the National Commission on the Causes and Prevention of Violence continues with this review of the efforts actually undertaken by the television industry:

> It is sufficient to note that although such promises (i.e., research) were made first in 1954 and continued through 1964, by October 1967 the amount of research sponsored by the industry on this issue was so small as to be insignificant, and that which was supported by the industry was, from the outset, clearly undertaken as a defensive move.[6]

With regard to the curtailment of programs depicting violence, the report goes on to note:

> Some studies in the files of the subcommittee indicate that the quantity of violent programs increased as much as 300 per cent between 1954 and 1961.

> After the tragic assassinations in the Spring of 1968, there was much publicity in the trade and regular press about how the networks were reducing violence on television. Content analysis conducted by the Media Task Force indicates that there was no such reduction by October, 1968.[7]

Criticism of children's television programs is not restricted to the issue of violence. Recent research by the new national organization

[6] *Violence and the Media: A Staff Report to the National Commission on the Causes and Prevention of Violence* (Washington, D.C.: U.S. Government Printing Office, 1969), p. vii.

[7] *Violence and the Media,* p. viii.

Action for Children's Television showed that two thirds of current television programs for children consist of chase-adventure cartoons. It is not being suggested here that chase-adventure cartoons are necessarily harmful to children; what is being pointed out is that such programs contribute little to the growth and development of the young. Such programs are rarely humorous or clever, and are frequently insulting to the viewer. To present these cartoons as children's programing is at best fraudulent. In reality they are relatively inexpensive fillers whose major purpose is to bombard children with countless "go after your parents" commercials. The commercials themselves are frequently misleading, with guarantees of power and prestige if only the child will purchase some brand of chewing gum, cereal, tooth paste, or soft drink.

The victimization and exploitation of our children is not always as apparent as it is in the case of the mass media. The current debate over the issue of I.Q. tests represents a more subtle, yet probably more insidious example of the way children suffer through the actions and behavior of even well-meaning, concerned adults.

Our purpose here is not to argue the merits or validity of I.Q. tests. There are already a sufficient number of scholars involved in that debate. It is clear also that while they continue their debate they have remained indifferent to the impact that their intellectual exchanges have had upon children. For while this debate rages, children continue to be labeled, categorized, and reminded that their failure to learn is not the fault of our schools or the methods by which we manipulate children but is due rather to their biological make-up, the incompetency or indifference of their parents, or their "social class."

The only ones to benefit from the I.Q. debate are the participating scholars (since it contributes to their prestige as productive scholars) and the educators who refuse to believe that the learning shortcomings of children might be explained by how and what they are taught. Any evidence that learning problems can be attributed to genetic factors, parental indifference, or ethnic and social class values will be readily endorsed by those who encounter difficulty with children. If the child fails, we do not look to the school. If the child is restless, we do not examine the content of the curriculum. If the child is angry, we do not study the impact of oppressive and frustrating rules and regulations. If the child fails, we do not send the teacher to summer school or deny salary payment. No, the child is the problem.

Even for those adults who are reluctant to hold the child totally responsible for his behavior, there is always an abundance of blame alternatives. The child may then be perceived as the unforunate recipient of an inferior culture or of inferior genes.

Still, no matter who is held responsible and whether or not there is consensus over the meaning of I.Q. tests the children are the victims, and the burden of proof continues to be placed upon them. Finally we might ask what difference does it make, anyway? Does it make a difference whether or not the nebulous quality we call intelligence is explained best by biological or by environmental factors? Will accounting in a methodologically approved fashion for the variations in human beings lessen the learning difficulties of children? Will agreeing that the cause is biological rather than environmental alter the fact that increasing numbers of children—I.Q. high tested and I.Q. low tested—are fed up with school at earlier and earlier ages? Will agreement among professors Jensen, Bruner, Kagan, Clark, and Herrnstein make any difference at all to the children? I think not.

THE EXPLOITATION OF THE AMERICAN GROWING CLASS

Peter B. Meyer

The national economy and its objectives, its institutions, and its implicit or explicit characterization of the family are all critical to the role experienced by children in a society. In arguing for a children's allowance in the United States, Daniel Moynihan has observed that ". . . it costs money to raise children . . . Men are paid for the work they perform on the job, not for the role they play in the family." [1] The accuracy, relevance, and importance of this statement are all specific to the characteristics of this socioeconomic system.

The first part of this essay, then, is a description of the context or background within which any view of children must be placed: the

[1] James C. Vadakin, *Children, Poverty and Family Allowances* (New York: Basic Books, Inc., Publishers, 1968), p. xii.

American socioeconomy as a whole and the role of the family and child within the national system. The second part of the essay deals explicitly with the economic role of children in America and includes evidence on the economic status of children in the nation. The final part indicates how the interplay between the socioeconomy and family structure leads to various forms of child exploitation.

THE ECONOMICS OF AMERICA

Many nations have become industrial and experienced urbanization in the process. The capitalist mode of production is found in most industrial economies, as is the prevalence of the nuclear family. However, only the United States combines an advanced economic state, a high degree of urbanization, an unfettered capitalist ethos, and socioeconomic reliance on the nuclear family with national "hugeness." These five elements of the American socioeconomy provide a frame of reference for a study of children in the United States.

The Advanced American Economy

No nation in the world can match the personal income *per capita* registered in the United States: $4,140 in 1971. We can point to myriad examples of our affluence, all derived from our relentless pursuit of physical or material accumulation. The national stress on material affluence has spawned our great herd of industrial behemoths and has sharply distorted the American child-rearing effort.

In presenting his Family Assistance Plan to Congress, President Nixon argued that the nation must make it possible for all persons "to contribute to the full extent of their capabilities," and thus has the obligation "of developing and improving those capabilities." [2] Those at the bottom of our socioeconomic ladder are supposed to be helped by an Office of *Economic Opportunity*. The national interest in in-

---

[2] "Welfare Reform: A Message from the President of the United States," House Document No. 91-146, *Congressional Record*, Vol. 115, no. 136, The House of Representatives, 91st Cong., 1st sess., 1969, H7241.

dividual development, then, appears to be focused on the potential economic gains for society to be garnered from particular forms of training for employment.[3]

The implications of such a focus for child-development spending are obvious: 29.9 percent of national personal income in 1969–1970 was taxed or levied directly on American families, but a mere 4.4 percent of income, collected primarily through indirect means, was spent on local elementary and secondary schools. Some basic training obviously contributes to economic growth, but the socioeconomy appears to be unwilling to pay the bills for broad-ranging child development.

Among the motivational tools accepted by the United States in its growth mania is the principle of payment based on work productivity. This principle is *not* inherent in a capitalist economy: in late nineteenth-century and early twentieth-century France, employers began to adjust wages to employees' family size. The French rejected the principle of equal pay for equal work in favor of a wage scheme that focused less on the worker than on the children who shared his lot. Family or children's allowances have now developed under government auspices in all industrialized capitalistic nations except the United States.[4] They pay varying amounts for each child or family member, normally to the mother of the children. In addition to the economic incentive basis for this nation's rejection of such a program, American attitudes toward the father's role as breadwinner have bolstered resistance to this children-oriented policy change.

Growth mania, then, has held down potential spending on education and child development in the United States while simultaneously limiting financial resources in many families to inadequate levels.[5]

[3] Economic arguments and the use of cost-benefit ratios for impact on national income are employed politically to support social change, since such arguments, and not those that focus on individuals and impacts on them, carry weight in the socioeconomy.

[4] See Vadakin, *Children, Poverty and Family Allowances,* for a good discussion of the rationale for, and evolution of, children's and family allowances in the industrialized Western world.

[5] At $1.60 an hour, the current minimum wage, a fully employed wage earner takes home less than $3,000 annually and can barely provide for a family of three. Many wage earners receive less than the minimum wage or work less than a full year and have families of four or more persons. Thus the need for supplemental children's allowances is extensive.

The Urbanized Nation

In 1970 less than one in twenty American families lived on a farm. Almost two thirds of all households lived in metropolitan areas with core cities of 50,000 or larger, and over half of them actually inhabited the center cities. Family incomes tend to rise with residential density, so urbanization continues to dominate American migration patterns.

Urbanization has facilitated provision of public and private services and access to professional specialists of all sorts at lowered costs because of the greater population densities. Specialization, which technologically has followed industrialization, has sociologically followed upon the urbanization that technological change first made possible and then fostered.

Specialization, and the perspectives derived from socioeconomic experience in a compartmentalized system, can be said to lie at the root of secondary school tracking, grouping of students into homogeneous classes, and other educational policies. Children are classified according to skill and interest to accommodate specialized teachers as well as to "improve" their learning experiences (and their future ability to specialize). Even in elementary school certain subjects are taught by specialized teachers. Each year the child in school meets a new person: the specialist in teaching a particular grade. Lessons with different specialists and a general damper on their enthusiasm for breadth of experiences, which are costly to provide, form the core of the developmental exposures of children in America's advanced, urbanized, specialized society.

The Capitalist Ethos

The United States subscribes to the purest exposition of the capitalist ethos as its economic rationale and self-description.

The essence of a capitalist economy is that production is not undertaken in pursuit of predetermined social goals, but rather because producers expect a profit from their activity. A simplistic characterization of the system would be *production for profit, not for use*. The capitalist ethos explains that consumers' wants are expressed as a willingness to buy, and that the use value of a product will be reflected in the profits to be made from its sale, so that production is determined by use value. This rationale ignores monopoly and oligopoly production and a critical facet of American capitalism: inequality. To the extent that some people do not have the income to express their consumption needs in dollar demands, production for profit differs from production for use, and the socioeconomy will fail to produce what the population in fact needs and desires.

As nonproducers in a system that rewards productivity, children depend upon their parents for income with which to articulate a consumption demand. This dependence is associated with a greater than average experience of poverty: 8.4 percent of all families consisting of two parents and their children had incomes per person under $1,000 in 1970, but 11.9 percent of the children in intact nuclear families fell into this extremely poor category. The presence and number of children in families contributes to increased incidence and severity of low incomes and poverty.[6] Thus families with children have had below-average per-person dollar votes to use in influencing production.

Another concomitant of the capitalist ethos as the basis for private and public decision-making is the irrelevancy to spending decisions of returns accruing specifically to children. The spending agent will calculate the returns to the socioeconomy of investment decisions in terms of production for sale and economic growth and, therefore, will consider the matter of personal returns to children as tangential.

The Role of the Nuclear Family

Since the probability of poverty grows for a family as the number of children within it rises, children are one source of poverty. Children dilute the family's income, and they tend to be born before that income has peaked; thus they share in a poverty that their families frequently "grow out of" through the sheer passage of time.

[6] In 1970, according to the Current Population Survey, 11 percent of all persons in families were poor, while 15 percent of children in families were poor. Families with one or two children exhibited an 8.5 percent poverty rate, while 13.3 percent of those with three or four offspring and 29.8 percent of those with five or more children were classified as poor. These relationships hold even with adjustments (upward) of the defined poverty lines. Data taken from U.S. Department of Commerce, Bureau of the Census, *Current Population Reports: Consumer Income,* "Poverty Increased by 1.2 Million in 1970," Series P-60, no. 77 (Washington, D.C.: U.S. Government Printing Office, 1971).

Little public or private intervention in what is frequently a temporary financial crisis in families is undertaken in the United States.[7] This lack of response may be attributed to a strong stress on the nuclear family and the paternal role as provider. A family allowance paid to the mother of a family is untenable in a social setting in which the father is to be both protector and provider. An automatic provision to *all* families, moreover, is in direct contradiction to the American emphasis on the ability of the nuclear family to stand alone.

The national stress on the independent nuclear family may, in part, be attributed to the growth of social programs that have weakened ties between older parents and their adult offspring. Social security, welfare, unemployment compensation, medicare, and the like form parallels to the social insurance provided by an extended family structure. If children in adulthood no longer are needed to provide for their parents, then the voluntary spending by parents on young children cannot be anticipated on the basis of traditional investment motives.

The "Hugeness" Ethic

Bigness is still largely equated with "goodness" in the United States. The critical ramification of this view of the world, which has characterized socioeconomic thinking in this nation for decades, is that the individual is less important than the organization since only the latter can attain hugeness.

Individual student differences are processed in such a manner as to facilitate increases in school and classroom size. Urbanization and increased population are common civic organization objectives. Corporate mergers, once frowned upon, accelerated during the 1960s. Admittedly the hugeness ethic has not increased family size, but family pursuits of bigger homes, bigger cars, and the like have depressed spending upon children.

Therefore, not only are children unimportant in that they do

---

[7] Although aid to dependent children has been one of the major income-maintenance programs in the United States for some time, such aid has, until recently, been limited to families with a single nondisabled adult. Only within the past decade has such assistance been extended to two-parent units with the major breadwinner unemployed. Payments are both very low and difficult to obtain—hardly a measure of a willingness to provide for poor families.

not produce, but the socioeconomy cannot view *any individual child* as significant. Individuality, and the development and encouragement of each person's uniqueness, then, are acceptable in the child-rearing process only insofar as is necessary to permit functional specialization in later life. Spending on children by both families and the public sector reflects this perspective.

AMERICAN CHILDREN: THEIR ROLE AND STATUS

Any discussion of the socioeconomic roles and status of children must consider the basic question of why people have children. A second issue is clearly why the socioeconomy earmarks dollars specifically for nonproductive children. The inequality that characterizes the system in these United States must also be considered a salient issue. These three questions are addressed in sequence below.

Children in the Family

Children in their pre-high-school years play no real productive role in the United States; they are consumers, or causes for consumption of goods and services by their parents. Children have become less and less important as a source of future economic security for their parents as social systems have replaced them. Why, then, do parents have children? Obviously some social pressure is brought to bear. Such pressures actually take two distinct forms. The first group of arguments dwells on the enjoyment that the parents (and perhaps predominantly the grandparents) will derive from their children. The second body of arguments is more nebulous but may be grouped together under the assumption that the bearing of society's young is the obligation of (married) adults.[8]

Taking the obligation arguments first, we can note that in adopting a policy of public provision of education the socioeconomy as a whole has accepted some public child-rearing obligations. The current debate over day-care for children centers in part on where the line dividing familial from societal obligations should be drawn. The sociomoral and economic issues raised are dealt with further below.

---

[8] Both religious anti-birth control beliefs and secular arguments against abortion may be classified into this second group of pressures.

The enjoyment arguments are, in a sense, a variant on the traditional reasons for having children. In agrarian societies dominated by extended family structures children act as producers at very early ages and later, as adults, provide for aging parents. In such societies, therefore, children may be said to be both current consumption and future investment goods in the eyes of their parents. In mechanized, urbanized, specialized, giantized America, with its dominant nuclear family structures, such reasons for having children are no longer significant. However, parallels can be drawn if the provision of entertainment, pleasure, and a sense of well-being to members of the family is considered a productive act. Young children can, and do, provide their parents with some measure of entertainment and pleasure (even if the latter is culturally conditioned) and are thus currently productive. Children serve an investment function as well, providing their parents some vicarious satisfaction in anticipating and observing future successes.

Parental attitudes toward children will determine the allocation of resources for them. In effect those attitudes will determine the value placed on what the children can produce. The capitalist ethos in the United States conditions people to relate on a *quid pro quo* basis, providing nothing unless some return is expected, and parental behaviors may be assumed to conform to this pattern. Parents may attempt to purchase avoidance of undesirable outputs (such as temper tantrums) so that spending may be partially correlated to child ability to manipulate parents. The *quid pro quo* relationship appears even in the most noncompetitive contexts, such as the threat "I will not take you to the circus unless you clean your room." (Perhaps the more "loving" American family may be defined as one in which parents and children bargain over such trades rather than deal on conditions laid down by the adults.) Granting, then, that parents expect some returns on their expenditures on children, the patterns of such spending may be examined.

Private medical expenditure levels are twice as high per person for adults as for the children's group.[9] Admittedly the incidence of

[9] Medical data taken from U.S. Department of Health, Education and Welfare, Social Security Administration, Office of Research and Statistics, *Research and Statistics Note*, "Health Care Outlays for Young, Intermediate and Older Age Groups," no. 17-1970, October 23, 1970, and U.S. Department of Health, Education and Welfare, Public Health Service, *Vital and Health Statistics*, "Children and Youth, Selected Health Characteristics, United States—1958 and 1968," Series 10, no. 62, February 1971.

deaths per 1,000 persons is higher for nineteen-to-sixty-four-year-olds than for those under eighteen, but the incidence of disability days lost to illness is comparable for both groups. Data point up an apparent lack of spending on preventive care. One child in every four between the ages of five and fourteen has never seen a dentist. Dental care for children is cosmetic and preventive; little of it is acute care or direct treatment. Apparently parental investment in reduced needs for future medical or dental care is not uniformly accepted as necessary by American families.

Expenditures on clothing by typical American households appear determined by age and sex.[10] Spending increases steadily with age, peaking for eighteen-to-twenty-four-year-olds, then declining somewhat, and dropping severely for those over sixty-five. The variation in spending on children may be attributed to several causes. The most obvious element is the price factor: smaller sizes cost less than larger ones in children's clothing. (The sixteen- to seventeen-year-olds have more spent on them than is spent on the twelve- to fifteen-year-olds largely because they may need adult, not children's, sizes.)

Spending on females appears comparable to outlays for males for children under the age of twelve but rises to 140 percent of spending on males for sixteen- to seventeen-year-olds. Children of twelve and over are much more apt to demand particular items of clothing than younger children, and girls, in our culture, are more likely to be pampered with "pretty things." Thus the pressures put on parents by their offspring for specific purchases is another element affecting spending. In summary it appears that price relationships determine parental outlays for minimum clothing *necessities,* but child pressure is a dominant determinant of the pattern of *discretionary* clothing spending.

Typical household budgets provide another view of the role of children in the family. The table below shows gross and net incomes, expenditure, estimated spending on children, and other elements of American family-of-four spending for three standards of living in 1967. Child-rearing expenses comprise less than half of the total

[10] Data from the 1960–1961 Consumer Expenditure Survey, as quoted in Ann Erickson, "Clothing the American Family: How Much for Whom?" *Monthly Labor Review,* 91, no. 1 (January 1968), 16, Table 1, show dollar spending on clothing as follows:

Age:	2–3	6–11	12–15	16–17	18–24	25–64	64+
Male	$67.49	$103.75	$144.02	$173.32	$184.52	$168.52	$77.16
Female	$73.98	$114.70	$186.99	$246.77	$255.17	$212.49	$97.73

INCOME AND SPENDING BY URBAN FAMILIES OF FOUR WITH THREE
DIFFERENT STANDARDS OF LIVING, URBAN U.S., 1967[a]

	LOWER STANDARD		MODERATE STANDARD		HIGHER STANDARD	
	$	% of Exp.	$	% of Exp.	$	% of Exp.
Gross Income	5,915		9,076		13,050	
Net Income	5,177		7,711		10,778	
Expenditures:	4,862		7,221		9,963	
On children[b]	2,209	(45.4)	3,198	(44.3)	4,326	(43.4)
On Education	44	(0.1)	55	(0.1)	64	(0.1)
On personal development	188	(3.9)	379	(5.2)	694	(7.0)
On child development	93	(1.9)	152	(2.1)	244	(2.4)

[a] Average of all urban areas for family consisting of employed father, housewife-mother, boy of thirteen, and girl of six.
[b] Estimated using other U.S. Government studies of family spending patterns under the assumption that one half of all spending on food and housing was attributable to the children.

SOURCE: U.S. Department of Labor, Bureau of Labor Statistics, *Three Standards of Living for an Urban Family of Four Persons, Spring, 1967,* Bulletin Number 1570-5, U.S. Government Printing Office, 1969.

family expenditures. The amount spent on children falls slightly as incomes rise, which lends credence to the contention that even wealthier parents do not, on average, pamper their children at their own expense.

Spending on education is minimal, and personal and child development are not major components of family spending. Less than one tenth of one percent of family expenditure is devoted to education. Since the data include families with children in *private* schools, this percentage is incredibly low. If one in forty of the moderate-income families pays $1,000 in private-school tuition, then each remaining household would be spending $5 on school supplies and fees for its two children. That is minimal indeed for a family earning over $9,000 per year.

Spending on personal development was calculated as the total of spending on education, recreation, and reading by the families. Such discretionary spending does rise with family incomes, but the children's share of the personal-development spending does not rise nearly as much as the total. It appears that *adult* development and personal growth is seen by most families to be more important than *child* development.

In conclusion, while nurturance is provided to children and standards of what constitutes adequate nurturance rise slightly with income, discretionary spending tends to be focused on adults, except insofar as children can force parental reallocations in their favor. In consonance with the lowered importance of the investment motive in child rearing, little attention is given to possible health or education problems that could emerge for children in the future.

Children in the Socioeconomy

Children are current contributors to this socioeconomy only insofar as they stimulate greater consumption than would exist in their absence. Children are, however, critical to the perpetuation of the nation. The socioeconomy as a whole, then, sees child rearing as crucial for assuring an adequate supply of producers and consumers in the future. The development of an ability to produce and consume is not, however, the development of a person to the highest level he or she can attain. Public effort is channeled: some children are "developed" more fully than others in order that the desired mix of labor skills be available. The setting of specific development targets shows up in the income inequalities discussed below.

The conditions under which children are raised have improved over the course of time—and children's standards of living may even have risen more rapidly than that of people in general. However, such "progress" needs to be examined closely to see if it represents a genuine concern for children as human beings or merely an interest in children as future participants in the socioeconomy.

The remarks of President Nixon before the White House Conference on Foods, Nutrition and Health exemplify the national frame of reference:

> A child ill-fed is dulled in curiosity, lower in stamina, distracted from learning. The cost of medical care for diet-related illness; remedial education required to overcome diet-related slowness in school; institutionalization and *loss of full productive potential*; all of these place a heavy economic burden on society as a whole.[11]

[11] Cited in U.S., Executive Office of the President, White House Conference on Children 1970, *Profiles of Children* (Washington, D.C.: U.S. Government Printing Office, 1970), p. 65.

The concern with productive potential and costs to the nation as a whole has been common to participants on both sides of the national debates on welfare reform, day care, educational development, and the like. A lack of focus on the children themselves has characterized almost all political discussion regarding their status and condition in the nation.[12]

Statistically we can observe that there has been an increase from 9 percent of total outlays to 11 percent in spending on children by the government over the past decade.[13] This increase in children's share of spending can, however, be at least partially attributed to an increase in the number of female-headed families, whose probability of poverty exceeds the norm and who are very likely to need help. Moreover, the increased spending, in and of itself, is not an indication of an increased concern for children.

National spending on public education below the college or university level has gone from 2 percent to 4 percent since 1946. Adult education's share of the outlay has risen from 3 percent to 12 percent, diluting the children's portion. More importantly, current outlays for administration and instruction rose five times, while capital outlay on physical plant climbed over twenty times. While we can be confident that physical school structures have improved somewhat, it is difficult to say that learning and child development have really been enhanced.

Alternatively we can look at need for social services. Needs for services have grown as the number of working mothers with preschool children has risen from three million to four million in the past decade. In the past twenty years the proportion of married women who join their husbands in the work force has risen from less than one fifth to over one third. Although the need for child care is becoming increasingly prevalent in intact families, not just broken ones, virtually no public provision has been made. Women continue to use neighbors and relatives and make other informal arrangements for child care. They cannot articulate the dollar demand needed to stimulate private child-development efforts. The public sector, in the po-

[12] An outstanding recent example is the fight over day care and child development between President Nixon, who vetoed a day-care bill, and the 92nd Congress, which focused on dollar costs and returns.

[13] Data taken from *Profiles of Children* and U.S., Executive Office of the President, *Economic Report of the President, Transmitted to Congress January 1972* (Washington, D.C.: U.S. Government Printing Office, 1972), Appendix B: "Statistical Tables Relating to Income, Employment and Production."

litical climate exemplified by voter rejection of new taxes for school financing, cannot fill the gap or provide funds to facilitate individual child development.

The lack of response of the socioeconomy as a whole to individual children's needs is best exemplified by the inability or unwillingness of the system to provide the resources needed by families for constructive nurturance of their young. Both social-service needs of families on all socioeconomic levels and the financial needs of units on the lower rungs of the socioeconomic ladder are ignored.

Income Inequality and Children

Three facets of inequality in the United States can be isolated and analyzed in terms of the condition of children. *Causality* is difficult to trace for all inequality, but some obvious cases can be identified. The *extent* of income inequality can be fairly clearly identified for private households, but inequality in public-service provision is not so obvious. Finally some generalizations can be made about the *impact* of inequality on children in America and their chances for full personal development.

Families headed by women are consistently poorer than families headed by men, which is not surprising given that the median income of female-headed families was less than 50 percent of that of male-headed ones.[14] Part of this differential is due to the fact that women are less than half as likely as men to have full-time jobs, but even among those families with fully employed heads the presence of a male in the house meant 50 percent more income on average. Each income earner beyond the first is worth between $2,000 and $3,000 to the average household, which is one reason why intact families are generally better off than units with a single adult. Families living in the South in 1970 received only about 85 percent of the national median family income. The typical black family received only three quarters of the average white family income.

It is therefore clear that the sex of the family head, the location of the family, the number of earners in the unit, and the race of the

[14] Data employed in this section, unless otherwise cited, are from U.S. Bureau of the Census, *Current Population Reports: Consumer Income,* "Income in 1970 of Families and Persons in the United States," Series P-60, no. 80, 1971.

household's members are all causal factors in income differences. What is much more blatant, however, is the range of income differences within any given type of family grouping. The wealthiest group is that of white families with both husband and wife in the labor force; their median income of $12,543 was 127 percent of the national family median of $9,867 in 1970. The wealthiest 5 percent of such units received a total income that was more than double what accrued to the poorest 20 percent of the households. While the poorest third of this group of families received a respectable $7,000 on average, the wealthiest third averaged better than $25,000. These differences are not due to family compositional characteristics; they may be partially attributed to education, but they are also influenced by factors totally external to the personal assets of family members: inherited wealth and property income.

Moving to consideration of all families in the United States, we can trace a consistent pattern of inequality in family income since 1947, with the poorest 20 percent of households in the nation receiving about 5 percent of all personal income and the wealthiest 5 percent receiving 15 percent. Inequality is slightly greater among nonwhites than whites and among families in the South than in the nation as a whole. These are two examples of a general pattern: income distribution inequality is more extreme among those subsets of families with low median incomes.

Families with household heads between the ages of 25 and 44 contain most of the children in the nation. These families exhibit some differences associated with the presence of children. Households with no children had a 1970 median income of $11,600. The presence of children reduced this median to $10,450, and the presence of children under the age of six had a further depressant effect, driving the median down to about $9,800. These differences in medians are amplified in terms of overall inequalities within and among the groups. Thus the children themselves who suffer from such inequalities, as demonstrated in the next paragraph, also contribute to their presence, however marginally.

So far we have avoided discussions of "poverty" as a measure of inequality since differences in family incomes can adversely affect all households. In appraising the impacts of inequality, however, it is appropriate to dwell on the poor as the most extreme case of such distributional effects. The impact of inadequate nutrition on children has been noted. The debilitating chain that can be initiated by severe malnutrition is virtually unbreakable for a minimum of two generations.[15] Health problems among the poor are not only more frequent but receive less care than is the case for the nonpoor. The incidence of decayed and untreated teeth in children between the ages of six and eleven, for example, has been found to fall as incomes rise.[16]

The impact of incomes on the physical well-being of children is just one measure of the consequences of inequality. The family and social dynamics initiated by poverty can induce further debilitation of children in terms of their self-images and ability to function in a competitive socioeconomy.[17] Patterns of status inheritance indicate that educational attainment on the part of children is the only factor that can consistently override the impact of parental social class. Unfortunately access to quality education is not equally distributed across families.

The South has been cited as the poorest area of the United States. Spending on education in the South in 1968–1969 averaged $618 per pupil, 83 percent of the national average of $834.[18] Such depressed education spending is a partial indicator that southern children have been shortchanged educationally. The tragedy of this finding is that the South was spending 7 percent of its personal income on elementary and secondary education, while the nation as a whole was only spending 6.5 percent. While allocating a proportionally greater share of its income to education, therefore, the South has still been unable to meet the national average because of its low level of income per person.

Between the patterns of private and public spending and the inequality inherent in both the social division of labor tends to replicate itself.[19] Children are investment goods to be embodied with those char-

[15] Peter B. Meyer and Penelope B. Pellow, *Patterns of Intergenerational Transfer of Poverty and Dependence: Techniques for Breaking the Cycle of Poverty,* Center for Human Services Development Report No. 4, 1971, College of Human Development, Pennsylvania State University, multilith.

[16] White House Conference on Children, *Profiles of Children,* p. 30, Chart 48.

[17] Meyer and Pellow, *Patterns of Intergenerational Transfer of Poverty and Dependence,* pp. 9–13.

[18] White House Conference on Children, *Profiles of Children,* pp. 168, 169, tables 136, 138.

[19] Melvin M. Fumin, *Social Stratification: The Forms and Functions of Inequality* (Englewood Cliffs, N.J.: Prentice-Hall, Inc., 1967); also Seymour M. Lipset and Rheinhard Bendix, *Social Mobility in an Industrial Society* (Los Angeles: University of California Press, 1959).

acteristics that will make them productive contributors in their adult years. Such embodiment is to be achieved at the lowest possible cost so as to attain the maximum possible return on the investment in training. Given the hierarchical production relationships of advanced industrial society, future workers will be trained for different jobs. Adherence to the capitalist ethos assures payment to workers in accordance with their productivity, which varies with the job. The lower returns accruing to some future workers logically call for lower expenditures on their education and development as children.

Efficiency has been the watchword of the American pursuit of so-called economic growth. In the name of efficiency children from poorer homes tend to be trained for lower-class jobs, since training them for upper-level jobs is not efficient in terms of returns on investment in training. The role of child-development agencies in society in reproducing the social division of labor can also be seen from examination of access to years of schooling. The probability of a child completing secondary school is positively related to the income level and years of education of his or her parents.[20] College attendance and graduation also follow this pattern. The share of the total educational resources allocated to each child from wealthier, better educated families, therefore, simply by virtue of his longer average tenure in the school system, will exceed that provided to each less advantaged child.

The inequality inherent in the provision of education gives the lie to the myth that the equalizing effects of free public education provide the critical counter to the disequalizing forces of capitalist labor markets. Since education mirrors other child development efforts, inequality in opportunity for personal development appears to characterize the United States today. Poorer children are not only stunted in terms of development but also in their prospects for status and income. Children from the upper class, however, also are stunted insofar as they are intentionally discouraged from developing skills and aptitudes (such as ability to work with hand tools) not appropriate to their predestined career tracks.

[20] Samuel Bowles, "Unequal Education and the Reproduction of the Social Division of Labor," *Review of Radical Political Economics,* 3, no. 4 (Fall–Winter 1971), 1–30. This article traces the development of free public education in the United States in response to labor market demands and identifies the major correlates of educational attainment in modern America.

THE EXPLOITATION OF AMERICAN CHILDREN

All funds allocated to children in the American socioeconomy can be attributed to an investment motive. The nurturance provided our children can be classified as a purely exploitative act: funds are provided so as to maximize the value received at some future date from children. While it may be argued that, in the same sense that such spending on children is exploitative, all spending on persons in our socioeconomy has an exploitative component, the strict dependency role of children creates special conditions.

Children do not participate in socioeconomic decisions either through direct control of dollar votes or through the ballot box. Decisions are made *for* them by persons in control of a socioeconomy that systematically excludes children as participants. The system uses children as perpetuators of a *status quo* that intentionally molds them from birth for future producer and consumer roles. The use of children as perpetuators of a socioeconomy that has acted to minimize their personal development and breadth of vision of possible change is clearly exploitative.

Considering poverty in the family to be a dominant factor in the perpetuation of social class differences, many analysts have called for income guarantees or other reallocational schemes designed to reduce or eliminate the experience of poverty by American households.[21] This line of argument fails to recognize the consistent patterns in all allocational decisions made within the socioeconomy.

As we have seen, the investment motive that governs public provision of services to children is conditioned by a rate-of-return computation. Thus, even if all households were to enjoy current income equality, however defined, child-development efforts would still strive to identify and capitalize on remaining socioeconomic class differences so as to facilitate minimum investment outlays. The child of

[21] Vadakin, *Children, Poverty and Family Allowances*; also Friedman, Milton, *Capitalism and Freedom* (Chicago: University of Chicago Press, 1962) and Robert Theobald, *Free Men and Free Markets* (New York: Clarkson and Tatten, 1953), both of whom envision social changes attendant to the provision of income guarantees. The literature through the middle of the 1960s has been ably surveyed by Christopher Green in his *Negative Income Taxation and the Poverty Problem* (Washington, D.C.: The Brookings Institution, 1967).

better educated parents would continue to enjoy an advantage in terms of probability of obtaining higher education. The child of white-collar workers would still be more likely than the offspring of blue-collar workers to be socialized into white-collar work. The child in a family of wealth holders and recipients of property income would still enjoy developmental advantages insofar as such wealth holding assured less income insecurity in the future.

Reduction of current family income inequality will not eliminate, or even greatly reduce, the exploitation of American children. The exploitative pattern experienced in the United States is conditioned by the hierarchical relationships that characterize the work place and by the central role played by the work place as a source of identity and status in the socioeconomy. Elimination of the exploitation of children, therefore, requires a leveling of the hierarchical relationships on which the socioeconomy has unnecessarily depended for maintenance of work motivation.[22]

In a more egalitarian socioeconomy, exploitation would be counterproductive in the work place, and the exploitation of children as future workers would cease to serve a constructive purpose. Such a system is not consistent with the unfettered pursuit of material gain by its component units nor can it be reconciled with a denigration of the individuals within it.

Exploitation of children can only be brought to an end in a socioeconomy in which the development of the individual is the highest social purpose and satisfaction of wants is understood to be possible in the absence of increased material production. It does not appear that such a socioeconomic system can evolve in the United States in the foreseeable future without major socioeconomic upheaval.

[22] Proof that efficiency does not necessarily require administrative hierarchies was developed by Seymour Melman in "Industrial Efficiency under Managerial vs. Cooperative Decision Making," *Review of Radical Political Economics*, 2, no. 1 (Spring 1970), 9–34.

CHILDREN AND
THE JUSTICE PROCESS:
REALITY AND RHETORIC

Daniel Katkin

The juvenile justice system created at the beginning of this century sought to abandon the traditional values of the criminal law. Retribution was to be replaced by love, justice by mercy, and punishment by treatment. That such a court was created tells us something about the special role of children in American society. Unfortunately, the children's courts, which were originally hailed as the best plan "for the conservation of human life and happiness ever conceived by civilized man," [1] matured into tribunals more awesome in the abuse of power

"Children and the Justice Process: Reality and Rhetoric," by Daniel Katkin. Copyright © 1973 by Daniel Katkin. This article appears for the first time in this book.

[1] Hoffman, "Organization of Family Courts, with Special References to the Juvenile Court," in *The Child, The Clinic, and The Court,* ed. J. Addams (New York: New Republic, Inc., 1927), p. 266.

than the Star Chamber.[2] That also tells us something about the special role of children in American society. We seem to care, but not to care enough.

Our concern is manifested by a proliferation of documents and studies about the plight of children in trouble;[3] our lack of concern is manifested by an inability to respond to the problem with sufficient resolve. As a people we spend in excess of $2 billion a year on pets, $9 billion a year on alcoholic beverages, and $36 billion a year on automobiles and automobile parts, but spend only a very small fraction of those amounts on meaningful programs to help youngsters who run afoul of the law.[4]

But the problems of the juvenile justice system are not merely problems of resources. There is something fundamentally wrong in the conception. For many years our zeal to "save" children led us to deny them many of the liberties to which our society believes individuals are entitled. More recently there has been substantial movement in the direction of awarding procedural rights to children; but in so doing we have come no closer to the ideal of special regenerative treatment for them. We seem unable to respond to our youngsters both as children with special needs and as people with equal rights.

In the first part of this essay the restrictive impact of the original juvenile court philosophy on the rights of children will be explicated. After that, the significance of recent Supreme Court decisions will be assessed. Finally, a partial answer will be attempted to the question: what special role should there be for a juvenile justice system?

JUVENILE COURT PHILOSOPHY AND THE RIGHTS OF CHILDREN

The reformers who crusaded to create the children's courts were parties to an intellectual revolution that may well be among the most

[2] R. Pound, Foreword to Young, *Social Treatment in Probation and Delinquency* (New York: McGraw-Hill Book Company, 1937), p. xxvii.

[3] For example, see H. James, *Children in Trouble: A National Scandal* (New York: Simon and Schuster, 1971); White House Conference on Children, *Report to the President* (Washington, D.C.: U.S. Government Printing Office, 1970); President's Commission on Law Enforcement and the Administration of Justice, *Task Force Report on Juvenile Delinquency* (Washington, D.C.: U.S. Government Printing Office, 1967).

[4] White House Conference on Children, *Report to the President,* p. 373.

important legacies of the nineteenth century. The generation before them believed that the universe is mysterious and incomprehensible; the generation after them believed that it is rational and that its mysteries can be unraveled. The transition took place during their lives with such events as the discovery of the atom, the promulgation of the theory of evolution, and the emergence of the social sciences. The reformers marched beneath the banner of scientific positivism, buoyed by the belief that human behavior is the product of antecedent causes and that knowledge of the causes permits planful intervention to facilitate behavioral change. Firm in the belief that they understood human behavior and that their knowledge gave them the power to change it, the reformers argued for the creation of a court based upon the rehabilitative ideal.

That the reform movement focused on the establishment of a special court for children rather than on radical modification of the techniques used to process adult offenders was no mere accident. The reformers were not only positivists, they were also child-savers. Their argument that juvenile offenders should be treated with special care was derived from two main considerations: (1) that children are not altogether responsible for their behavior and (2) that the state has an affirmative duty to help "socialize" children.

1. Childhood and Responsibility

The criminal law has always recognized that it is inappropriate to punish people who are not responsible for their behavior. Punishment is appropriate only for those who are culpable and blameworthy. The label "criminal" is not affixed to all those who harm others but only to those whose harmful acts are purposeful. Thus it is that accidents are not crimes,[5] that insanity is a defense against a criminal accusation,[6] and that the criminal prosecution of children under the age of seven has never been permitted.[7] The reformers, knowing that children do not magically become mature or responsible at seven, merely argued for an extension.

[5] See, for example, *Fain v. Commonwealth,* 78 Ky. 183, 39 Am. Rep. 213 (1879).
[6] See A. Goldstein, *The Insanity Defense* (New Haven: Yale University Press, 1967).
[7] V. Stapleton and L. Teitelbaum, *In Defense of Youth* (New York: Russell Sage Foundation, in press).

Their argument was strengthened by the developing body of social scientific theory that patterns of human behavior are molded in childhood by environmental conditions. In this view the delinquency of a child is primarily evidence of parental failure. A child in trouble with the law does not deserve punishment and will not benefit from it. Rather, he deserves (as all children deserve) warm, loving, solicitous care and custody. If a child's parents are unable or unwilling to provide such care and custody, then the state must intervene *on his behalf*.

2. The State as Parent

To the reformers, the manner in which society responds to youthful misconduct was not primarily an issue of penology or of criminal law; it was part of the broader problem of creating a utopian social order. If education could be converted from the "sterile" dissemination of a certain body of information to a means of adjusting men "in a healthful relation to nature and their fellowmen," so the system of justice, at least as applied to children, could also be made to serve the same end.[8]

Thus, state intervention in the juvenile courts was not intended to further such traditional penological values as retribution and deterrence; rather it was to provide children with the type of care they might receive at the hands of "wise" parents.

Judge Julian Mack, an early incumbent of the Chicago juvenile court bench, summarized this position as follows:

There is a . . . [fine and noble] legal conception hidden away in our history that . . . [should be] invoked for the purpose of dealing with the youngster that has gone wrong. That is the conception that the State is the higher parent; that it has an obligation, not merely a right but an obligation, to step in when the natural parent, either through viciousness or inability, fails so to deal with the child that it no longer goes along the right path that leads to good, sound, adult citizenship.[9]

This "noble" conception, generally referred to as the *parens patriae* doctrine, was the major assumption around which the juvenile

[8] Stapleton and Teitelbaum, *In Defense of Youth*, p. 15.
[9] J. Mack, "The Chancery Procedures in the Juvenile Court," in *The Child, The Clinic, and The Court*, ed. J. Addams, pp. 311–12.

justice system was constructed and the major justification for the general diminution of the procedural rights accorded to youngsters. After all, the relationship between a parent and child—even an erring child —cannot be regulated by the same rules that apply in a felony prosecution involving an adult. The nation's appellate courts accepted this logic and ruled that juvenile court proceedings were not criminal in nature.

> The natural parent needs no [due] process to temporarily deprive his child of its liberty by confining it in its own home, to save it and to shield it from the consequences of persistence in a career of waywardness, nor is the state, when compelled, as *parens patriae,* to take the place of the father for the same purpose required to adopt any process as a means of placing its hands upon the child to lead it into one of its courts.[10]

Such decisions freed the juvenile courts from the traditional due-process restraints that are at the core of American criminal procedure.

Defense attorneys became, at best, infrequent participants in juvenile courts. The proceedings were conceptualized as neither criminal nor adversary,[11] therefore the participation of an attorney did not seem to the reformers to be necessary. Indeed such a presence might even detract from the desired informal and therapeutic relationship between the child and the court.

Similarly the privilege against self-incrimination (guaranteed in criminal prosecutions by the fifth and fourteenth amendments) did not have much force in the juvenile courts. No doubt the reformers felt that the privilege would undermine the very nature of the juvenile courts. After all, the judge was viewed primarily as a clinician, and successful therapy is impossible with a child whose response to questions is: "I plead the fifth."

For similar reasons jury trials were not permitted in juvenile court. The reformers' aim was to allow no agency—lawyers, the fifth amendment, or even juries—to stand between the child and the court. It was feared that the presence of a jury would make informality impossible and might even undermine the confidentiality of the proceedings. Furthermore, the *parens patriae* doctrine lent itself to an argument against the use of juries. As one court put it, "whether the child

[10] *Commonwealth v. Fisher,* 213 Pa. 48, 53, 62 Atl. 198, 200 (1905).
[11] See Stapleton and Teitelbaum, *In Defense of Youth,* p. 31, n. 56.

deserves to be saved by the state is no more a question for the jury than whether the father, if able to save it, ought to save it." [12]

Similar propositions were invoked to permit a relaxation of the usual role that convictions be based upon *proof beyond a reasonable doubt.* Juveniles could be adjudicated delinquent upon less sufficient evidence. Judge Ben Lindsey of the Denver juvenile court justified this procedure as follows:

> The whole proceeding is in the interest of the child and not to degrade him or even to punish him. We do not protect the child by discharging him because there is no legal evidence to convict, as would be done in a criminal case when we know that he has committed the offense. This is to do him a great injury, for he is simply encouraged in the prevalent opinion among city children . . . that it is all right to lie all they can, to cheat all they can, to steal all they can, so long as they "do not get caught" or that you have "no proof." [13]

It is important to note that the erosion of the rights of children was neither gradual nor malicious. Due process of law simply was not compatible with the humanitarian zeal of the founders of the juvenile justice system. Thus, in pursuit of the rehabilitative ideal, the ideal of justice came to be largely canceled out.

It was the lack of justice combined with doubts about the extent to which rehabilitation had actually been realized by the juvenile courts that occasioned the landmark decision of the Supreme Court in *In re Gault.*[14]

LEGAL REVISION

Fifteen-year-old Gerald Gault was adjudicated delinquent because he made an obscene telephone call. His trial took place without any notice of the charges ever having been given either to him or to his parents. The family was never advised of a right to counsel. In addition, the woman who claimed to have received the obscene call was not present at the hearing and thus could not be cross-examined.

[12] *Commonwealth v. Fisher,* 213 Pa. 54, 62 Atl. 200 (1905).

[13] B. Lindsey, "The Juvenile Court of Denver," in *Children's Courts in the United States,* ed. S. Barrows (Washington, D.C.: U.S. Government Printing Office, 1904), p. 107.

[14] 387 U.S. 1 (1967).

Furthermore, Gerald was questioned by the judge without having been advised of the privilege against self-incrimination. An adult guilty of the same offense could receive a maximum punishment of two months imprisonment or a fine of between five and fifty dollars; young Gault, however, after adjudication, was committed to the State Industrial School for a period that might extend until his twenty-first birthday.

Gerald's family attacked the constitutionality of the ajudication in the Supreme Court of Arizona, but they were unsuccessful. That court stood four-square on traditional juvenile court philosophy. Prior notice of the exact charge was said to be unnecessary because "the policy of the juvenile law is to hide youthful errors from the full gaze of the public and bury them in the graveyard of the forgotten past." [15] The absence of counsel was said to be inconsequential because "the parent and the probation officer may be relied upon to protect the infant's interest." [16] And the denial of the privilege against self-incrimination was found to be proper because "the necessary flexibility for in-dividualized treatment" would be enhanced by it.[17]

On all three points the Arizona court was reversed by the Su-preme Court. *In re Gault* stands for the proposition that juveniles must be accorded "the essential of due process and fair treatment." [18] The logic underlying the opinion is of particular importance.

In large measure the decision seems to be based on the view that the juvenile justice system has not satisfactorily fulfilled the responsi-bilities imposed upon it by the *parens patriae* doctrine. The court pointed out that the claim of confidentiality has been "more rhetoric than reality";[19] it maintained that the adjudicatory process has been confusing and anti-therapeutic.[20] Perhaps most important, the court found that the institutions to which juveniles are remanded fall far short of the standards suggested by the rehabilitative ideal:

> Ultimately . . . we confront the reality of that portion of the juvenile court process with which we deal in this case. A boy is charged with misconduct. The boy is committed to an institution where he may be restrained of liberty for years. It is of no consti-

[15] *Application of Gault,* 99 Ariz. 181, 407 p. 2d 760 (1966).
[16] *Application of Gault,* 99 Ariz. 190, 407 p. 2d 767.
[17] *Application of Gault,* 99 Ariz. 191, 407 p. 2d 767–8.
[18] 387 U.S. 30.
[19] 387 U.S. 24.
[20] 387 U.S. 26.

tutional consequence—and of limited practical meaning—that the institution to which he is committed is called an Industrial School. The fact of the matter is that, however euphemistic the title, a "receiving home" or an "industrial school" for juveniles is an institution of confinement in which the child is incarcerated for a greater or lesser time. His world becomes "a building with white-washed walls, regimented routine and institutional laws. . . ." Instead of mother and father and sisters and brothers and friends and classmates, *his world is peopled by guards, custodians, state employees, and "delinquents" confined with him for anything from waywardness to rape and homicide.*[21]

All of this implies that had the juvenile justice system been truer to its mission, the results in *Gault* might never have obtained. In essence the Supreme Court declared that the informal procedures used by the juvenile courts were no longer permissible because the bedrock to which they were anchored—the notion that the state was functioning as a parent—was illusory rather than real. Due-process rights were extended to children only when it became undeniably clear that the humanitarian ideals of the juvenile court reformers had not been realized.

We seem unable to respond to our youngsters both as children with special needs and as people with equal rights.

Yet that is an aspiration worth striving toward, and it is still possible that the juvenile court might become a forum in which it could be attained.

A SPECIAL ROLE FOR THE JUVENILE COURT

The ideal of equal rights plus special treatment cannot be attained in the juvenile courts alone; it is dependent upon reform in all the institutions that serve children in trouble. And such reform, of course, can be won only if there is a real commitment to it, manifested in a willingness to allocate scarce resources. Nevertheless, the juvenile courts, by strict adherence to the ideal, can offer children a special type of solicitous care that could not be available in regular courts despite their commitment to due process. *In re Edwin R.*, a New York City case, is illustrative.[22]

[21] 387 U.S. 27 (emphasis added).
[22] 323 N.Y.S. 2d. 909 (1971).

Five youngsters were involved in the case. They were charged with the fatal stabbing of another youngster, an act that if performed by an adult would constitute the crime of murder. A series of pre-trial motions, raised primarily by the defense attorneys, caused the actual hearing to be put off for two years. When the trial finally began the youngsters' lawyers moved to dismiss the petition on the ground that the boys were no longer in need of any rehabilitative treatment that the court might be able to offer.

Social workers, psychiatrists, and educators testified that during the intervening years the boys had made a good adjustment. It was not argued that the boys were now model citizens, but only that they were making reasonable progress in that direction. The court took the position that its power to adjudicate a child delinquent is dependent not only upon the commission of some delinquent act, but also upon the child's need for "supervision, treatment, or confinement." [23] Because these children no longer seemed to have such need, the court granted the motion to dismiss the petition.

Such a result in a criminal court dealing with adult offenders would be unimaginable. Such courts are concerned not primarily with the welfare of the offender, but with such traditional penological values as deterrence, social protection, and retribution,[24] each of which demands that those who commit murder receive some sort of punishment. In dismissing the petition in *In re Edwin R.*, Judge Guerreiro elevated the rehabilitative ideal to special proportions in the juvenile court.

> The Family Court is not a Criminal Court with punitive objectives. The purpose of this court is to rehabilitate children and to make services available to them, not to vindicate private wrongs.[25]

The importance of the decision in *In re Edwin R.* derives not from the power of the court that decided the case (for decisions of the Family Court of New York City have no binding precedential effect in any other court) but from the logic of the opinion. In an era dominated by the decision in *In re Gault* and by a concern for vindicating the rights of juveniles, the opinion in *In re Edwin R.* points the

[23] 323 N.Y.S. 2d. 911.

[24] See Note, "Appellate Review of Primary Sentencing Decisions: A Connecticut Case Study," *Yale Law Journal,* 69 (1960), 1453, 1455.

[25] *In re Edwin R.,* 323 N.Y.S. 2d. 911 (1971).

way for the juvenile courts to be something more than institutions of criminal justice. Read together, these two cases suggest that it may yet be possible to establish a children's court with a special mission not only to care for children, but also to protect their liberty.

SUMMARY

The thesis of this essay is that children are entitled to be treated not only with due process of law, but also with the solicitous care and regenerative treatment postulated by the child-savers who founded the juvenile court movement. The creation of a juvenile court system that actually fulfills both functions ought to have a high priority amongst those with a genuine concern for the welfare of children. However, a contemporary movement for reform ought to proceed with caution, for one thing emerges clearly from history: that the path to hell is indeed paved with good intentions.

Part Two: Perspectives

EMERGENCE OF IDENTITY

From the White House Conference on Children (Forum 2)

To discuss the problems of emergence of identity, some common understandings about the meaning of "identity" are important. In the behavioral science literature, having a sense of identity has come to mean being able to answer satisfactorily the questions, "Who am I?" and "Where am I going?" Some would add, "Where did I come from?" The "Who am I?" includes knowing what I can do, what I am unable to do, what kind of person I am, and what is my best way of doing things. The "Where am I going?" includes an understanding of such things as what I can become, what I can learn to do, what I cannot learn to do, and what I want to become.

A strong sense of identity, however, is not enough. What is

"Emergence of Identity." From *Report to the President: White House Conference on Children* (Washington, D.C.: U.S. Government Printing Office, 1970).

needed is a healthy sense of identity—one both favorable and realistic. The following characteristics have been attributed to the person with a healthy sense of identity:

- A feeling of being in one piece, with an integrated rather than confused or diffused self-concept
- Certainty about one's place in the world and about how to behave
- Autonomy as a person and confidence in self, ability to establish and maintain independent judgments without reference to external sources
- Insistence upon being oneself rather than playing at being oneself
- High capacity for empathy and for respecting the identity of others

There are many types of identity—family, ethnic and cultural, religious, political, economic, physical, sexual, and intellectual. Identity involves all aspects of a person's being. Research during the past few decades has firmly established the validity of the concept of the uniqueness of each individual. And more recent evidence strongly indicates that the foundation for this individual unique identity is established in the early years.

To fully realize one's human potential, each person must have a strong, healthy identity and must recognize, acknowledge, and respect the identity of others in the same terms. Today we fall short on both counts, often because broad discrepancies exist between common social practices and knowledge about individuality. Many children develop both unfavorable and unrealistic identities; many lack virtually any identity.

Several workshops tried to formulate new and more satisfying definitions of identity. Some of the more interesting ones are listed below.

- My identity depends upon my knowing who I am, where I came from, who I may become and how I relate to others. Therefore, when I am young and helpless, people must give me what I must have to be aware, alert, healthy, and secure. I have a good identity if I know people like me, if people respect me, if I can do most of the things that are important to me—then, when I am old enough to know what I want to do with my life, I hope to live my life. I hope to live in and help shape a society that will give me that chance.

- Identity is a uniquely human characteristic which is a natural by-product of human experience. From birth (and before) a baby has a mind and experiences a private consciousness. The infant must relate as a separate being to things in the universe. The essence of human identity does not rest in ethnicity, language, sex, religion, or material surroundings. These are only variables of identity which can and do change—sometimes quite rapidly. The essence of identity is a person's capacity to think and to feel—to be a conscious being.

- Identity is the totality of one's thoughts and feelings about the universe—one's self, one's surroundings, others, and the unknown. As a child develops, he or she will become aware of and relate to more and more of a personal universe. The child will develop a positive, healthy identity only if capacities to think and feel are guided toward knowledge and love. Knowing and loving must expand with awareness, and a child must come to know and to love self and others. Only if these capacities continue to expand will the child be able to fulfill his or her human potential and become his or her true self. If this expansion of knowledge or love is frustrated or blocked, the child will remain unhappy, unsatisfied, even disturbed.

- If a child is to be equipped to continue to grow and develop a strong, healthy identity, he or she will have a positive attitude toward those things that he or she does not know. A child must learn to love the unknown and must be comfortable with infinity. He or she must become attracted to this unknown in himself or herself, in others, and in the universe itself.

- We believe that every human being has a right to optimally develop his potentialities. Every person is unique and each has his own potentialities, goals, precepts, liabilities, and assets. Society's task, then, is to help each child, without force or pressure, to grow in relationship to his uniqueness and to become a productive member of society.

Perhaps the dominating concern of the 1970 White House Conference on Children was to reaffirm the value of children. This concern has arisen because in America many adults have become separated, almost imperceptibly but surely, from the everyday lives of children. The worlds of childhood and adulthood must be more effectively meshed so children may both learn about, and try on, a variety of grown-up experiences; and so adults may share their children's dreams, thoughts, joys, disappointments, and, indeed, their playfulness. Understanding a child's developmental tasks is fundamental to drawing together adults and children. Such understanding can also reform and refocus both old and new programs designed for children and their families.

This report considers factors which enhance or impede the development of a child's sense of identity and suggests ways of ensuring that each child has the maximum opportunity for developing his own functional, healthy sense of identity—whatever his cultural, ethnic, or social background.

The phrase "emergence of identity" emphasizes the creative, self-acting nature of human beings and implies that in the early years a child's sense of identity comes about unaided, and, in a sense, this is just what happens. Yet many things can happen to prevent a child from developing a sense of identity or to cause him to develop an unfavorable and unrealistic sense of identity.

Initially, the infant has no conscious sense of self and cannot differentiate between "me" and "not me." The beginnings of a sense of self originate in the infant's body through countless experiments involving touch, sight, hearing, smell, and movement. Gradually the notion dawns that things exist outside oneself.

Another aspect of identity emerges with a change in the infant's attachment to the predominant person or persons in his or her life from one based on need and need gratification (during the first six months) to one of love, largely independent of need gratification (second six months). The infant's sense of identity continues to emerge as he learns that certain actions elicit response from his environment.

Attaining the physical skill of creeping firmly establishes the infant's sense of separateness. Creeping enables him to discover and rediscover objects and learn that objects exist independently of his subjective experience. He begins to understand that people and things follow their own laws and not his, although he also begins increasing his repertoire of skills for controlling both people and things. He begins naming things and asking the names of new things encountered, a sign that he is aware of himself as one object among other objects.

By the time he is two and one-half years a child knows "I" and "you." He has learned that he is a person. He is now ready for the task of learning his sex identity. During his third, fourth, and fifth years, he begins to learn his family, ethnic, religious, economic, physical and athletic, and intellectual identity. This learning becomes increasingly complex depending upon the nature of the child's individuality and the way the environment treats it. The average three-year-old, for example, may learn little about his intellectual identity. Yet the intellectually gifted three- or four-year-old who begins reading without instruction may learn a great deal about it. Even if his parents try to prevent others from knowing that he reads, the child will learn that his accomplishment is unusual from his peers or adults who witness his verbal skills. If a child successfully accomplishes these multiple and demanding developmental tasks, he will have a firm beginning sense of identity by the age of six.

The work of Forum 2 cannot be fully understood without knowing something of how its recommendations have emerged. Before the task force met, the Chairman prepared a background paper delineating the issues and summarizing research information about them. In its first series of meetings, task force members listed problems regarding identity emergence during the early years, formulated ideas about how various persons might facilitate emergence of healthy identities, and proffered some ideas about how these persons might be educated to perform these roles. These problems were discussed from multiple viewpoints since the task force members, coming from immensely diverse backgrounds, included an Indian public health physician, a social worker, a child psychologist, a cartoonist, a religious educator, and a designer of child environments, to name but a few.

The task force identified the following major obstacles to the emergence of strong healthy identities:

- Deprivation (economic, pyschological, social, cultural)
- Sex discrimination and overemphasis on socially determined sex differences unrelated to sexuality
- Ethnic, racial, and religious prejudice and discrimination
- Taboos against acceptance of biological identity

- Taboos against acceptance and expression of affection
- Failure to learn skills of mastery and competence
- Overemphasis on conformity and uniformity with a resultant discrepancy between a healthy identity and a functional identity

The task force generally agreed that parents are the most important mediators of these influences, but that even brief contacts with the following persons may also strongly influence emergence of identity in the early years:

- Workers in day care centers
- Workers in church nurseries and other religious organizations that work with children
- Pediatricians and pediatric nurses
- Child psychologists and child psychiatrists
- Welfare workers
- Writers of children's books, comic strips, television shows, films, etc.

Ideas for action by each of these groups were produced by Forum members.

- Workers in community agencies
- Architects, toy designers, environmental designers
- Lawyers, judges, etc.
- Trainers of personnel for nurseries, day care centers, kindergartens, and child development centers

In the second series of Forum meetings, the task force recognized that the emergence of identity in the early years is largely influenced by certain harmful cultural assumptions widespread in the United States. These cultural assumptions must be changed to reflect existing knowledge about the nature of man and human development. Some existing assumptions and their more valid alternatives are listed below.

Current Cultural Assumptions	*Alternative Cultural Assumptions*
• Man is innately evil.	• Man is born neither good nor bad but with dignity and innate potential for

Current Cultural Assumptions

Alternative Cultural Assumptions

largely determining his "human" development.

- Giving attention to "inadequate" behavior motivates "adequate" behavior.

- Attending "adequate" behavior motivates "adequate" behavior.

- The good child is a modest child.

- Recognition and acceptance of positive characteristics are necessary for self-realization.

- Suffering produces character and prevents spoiling.

- Coping positively and constructively with developmental and emergency problems is healthy.

- Independent behavior is the behavior necessary to achieve personal and cultural competence.

- Interdependent behavior is the road to cultural competence and interpersonal satisfaction. Dependence is natural and healthy; it will diminish with increasing maturity.

- Competition is a behavior innate to the nature of man. (The only way one man can rise is to best someone else.)

- Each individual is unique and has particular strengths which must be valued.

- There is a superior race and/or set of cultural characteristics to be emulated. (Too much difference weakens the American way of life.)

- There is no superior race, sex, or set of cultural characteristics. Accept qualitative human differences without judging superiority or inferiority.

- Parenthood is essential to male and female actualization.

- Parenthood is only one socially acceptable alternative life style.

- Expression of feelings demonstrates weakness.

- Expression of feelings is essential to mental health.

- Genetics is the factor that

- Genetics provides the basis

Current Cultural Assumptions	*Alternative Cultural Assumptions*
determines what one is and what one can become.	for behavior, interacting with the internal and external environment.

It is not suggested that these assumptions and their alternatives exist as sharp dichotomies. Rather they should be thought of as part of a continuum.

This list is tentative and was not unanimously accepted by the Forum, although the delegates agreed that we need to reappraise our cultural assumptions and search for more valid ones.

When Forum task force members and delegates met during the Conference, an attempt was made to create an atmosphere that would stimulate creative problem solving. To facilitate this process, a group of process experts and content experts worked together to enable the total Forum, as well as workshop groups, to communicate and make decisions without using formal, parliamentary procedure. Such positive, communicative informality gave all delegates a chance to express their views in a way which would not have been possible under more formal procedures.

To stimulate delegates' thinking in terms of what the child experiences as he forms his identity so that recommendations would be relevant and implementable at the Federal, state, local, and personal levels, a series of pre-discussion activities was devised. These included experiences dealing with the emergence of identity through movement; a trip through a "Tree House" environment, designed to aid delegates in intimately experiencing the world of the infant, the world of stress and strain of the young child, and the world of young children's play and worship; and a video laboratory in which eight television screens simultaneously displayed the behavior of eight different children of different ages ranging from three months to three and one-half years.

These "opening up" experiences also enabled delegates to freely express their feelings. Many Forum members had feelings of frustration, doubt, anger, and fear, particularly fear that no government action would be taken on recommendations. To deal with these frustrations, one group took positive action in the form of a march for children to the White House, and another group recommended that no Conference recommendations be government processed until an independent office of child advocacy was established. As communication continued, however, the Forum delegates decided against refusing to submit a formal report, but to follow the previously described structure and submit recommendations. The total Conference experiences brought delegates new insights about themselves, about ways of working creatively and productively in small and large groups, and working both with and outside "the established system." Such insight may be a truly important serendipitous outcome of the Forum's emergence of identity.

In developing their report and formulating their final recommendations, the delegates considered such topics as infant individuality, family influences, the effect of failure, motility, the development of intelligence, and identity emergence in disadvantaged children.

The report of the 1950 White House Conference on Children and Youth pointed out that children of all ages manifest a high degree of individuality. Even newborn infants differ not only in physical characteristics such as weight and height, but also in their reactions to environmental stimuli. The report recognized, however, the acute scarcity of empirically tested knowledge concerning individual differences among children.

Although empirically established information about the individuality and emergence of identity among children below age six is still scarce, significant data have been collected since 1950. Thomas, Birch, Chess, Hertzig, and Korn demonstrated that children can be identified by styles of functioning at very early ages. Their study also implies that all infants will not respond in the same fashion to the same environmental influence and that child-rearing practices have different behavioral results depending upon the child's nature. The study questions attempts to apply the same rules to all children and stresses that each child's primary reaction pattern should be understood and respected.

The more important social forces affecting the child's development and emergence of identity include the family, the family constellation, the peer group, and other significant people. The family represents an ethnic background, a religion, and a social status. The child is even affected by the father's occupation, since it tends to place him in a certain cultural context. The child's experiences within the family develop his sense of acceptance or rejection.

The availability of parental identity figures also seems critical in the emergence of identity. Clinicians often observe that young people and adults with serious identity problems lacked appropriate identity figures during childhood. Early identity patterns acquired through imitation, incorporation, and identification with parental figures, however, may impose powerful inhibitions upon subsequent activity and structural differentiation in other areas. For example, potential talent may be blocked from extensive development by such deep-laid self-concepts.

To facilitate the emergence of strong, healthy identities and foster creative potentialities, family interaction should have the following characteristics:

- Families should create conditions that encourage curiosity, exploration, experimentation, fantasy, questioning and testing the limits, and development of creative talents.
- They should provide opportunities for developing the skills of creative expression, creative problem solving, and constructive response to stress and change.
- They should prepare family members for new experiences and help them develop creative ways of coping with them.
- They should find ways of transforming destructive energy into constructive, productive behavior rather than relying upon punitive methods of control.
- They should find creative ways of resolving conflicts between the needs of any two family members.
- Every family member should be given individual attention and respect and the opportunities to make significant, creative contributions to the welfare of the family as a whole.
- Families should imaginatively use community resources as well as supplement the community's efforts.
- Family interaction should provide purpose, commitment, and courage.

There is consensus that the emergence of a healthy sense of identity is damaged by continuous failure and by situations in which the child senses that he is "less than others." A growing body of evidence favors emphasizing a child's strengths instead of stressing his weaknesses and insisting that he overcome them. Discouragement and a feeling of hopelessness seem especially debilitating and may stem from a lack of confidence in one's capacity to cope with problems.

Movement can be a prime motivating force for young children

and can offer opportunities for exploration and achievement. White's study on "The Concept of Competence" establishes that motility is a drive in its own right and feelings of competence are dependent, in part, on opportunities for movement exploration.

Rowen believes that it is natural for children to use movement in the first years of life for creative expression. She believes further that, since movement is an early expression of children's creativity, it can be used to cultivate and keep alive their creative impulses so they can be carried into adult life with heightened power.

Since the last White House Conference, much evidence has been accumulated concerning the impact of the child's first years of life on his later functioning. From several studies, J. McV. Hunt has assembled evidence to discredit the following concepts about the nature and measurement of intelligence:

- A belief in fixed intelligence
- A belief in predetermined development
- A belief in the fixed and static, telephone-switchboard nature of brain function
- A belief that experience during the early years, and particularly before the development of speech, is unimportant
- A belief that whatever experience does affect later development is a matter of emotional reactions based on instinctual needs
- A belief that learning must be motivated by homeostatic need, by painful stimulation, or by acquired drives based on one of these

Early care exerts very powerful influences on a child. Existing studies indicate that, when deprived of early care, a child's development is almost always retarded—physically, intellectually, and socially.

The first years of life were investigated by Skeels in his "Iowa Studies" of the 1930's. Almost by chance Skeels discovered that two orphaned infants who had been personally cared for by mentally retarded adolescent girls showed unexpected spurts in development. Skeels and Dye then arranged a study in which retarded adolescent girls cared for 13 infants who were failing to thrive in an orphanage environment. At the time of transfer, the babies were about 19 months old and had a mean IQ of 64. A comparison group of 12 infants was found, averaging 16.6 months of age and having a mean IQ of 86.7. After an experimental period of 19 months, the children receiving personal attention from retarded adolescent girls showed an average IQ gain of 28.5 points, while the comparison group in the orphanage, after an average interval of 30.7 months, lost 26.2 IQ points. Skeels' work has been reinforced by Benjamin Bloom, who also stressed the importance of the first years of life for intellectual development.

Our society, with its emphasis on power and wealth, has neglected its most valuable resource, children. Strangely, however, we have failed to count the cost of this neglect. In the Skeels study described above, the institutionalized children having primarily custodial care continued to cost society throughout their lives, while the similar children who experienced human affection during their early years lived outside institutions and became contributing members of society. In terms of 1963 money values, Skeels estimated that one case placed in the institution had cost the state $100,000. If we multiply this figure by the current number of delinquent, mentally ill, and unemployable children, the cost of neglect to society becomes staggering.

Another aspect of research in the 1960's focused on the child who grows up in severe economic, cultural, and educational deprivation. This research has generally emphasized the intellectual deficits of disadvantaged children, and corrective programs have been compensatory in nature.

It is generally agreed that race and minority group awareness emerge in very early childhood and powerfully affects the emergence of a healthy identity. One of the most remarkable developments of the past decade has been moves by black, red, and brown groups in the United States to create more healthy identities based on this early race awareness. The more positive leaders of these movements stress the positive aspects of their racial identities and the contributions of members of their races. Most of these leaders deplore the sameness implied in equality and call for either recognition of those aspects of their own cultures they regard as superior—or at least the right to retain these features.

Woodward has presented a provocative and persuasive rationale for "Black Power" and "Achievement Motivation." He believes that Black Power is a useful conceptual framework for understanding the high achievement of those Afro-Americans who have overcome seemingly impossible odds to lead highly productive lives. Such reflections of the Black Power concept as James Brown's popular song, "Say it loud, I'm Black and I am proud!" have done much to foster a new kind of identity among Blacks.

Sensitive observers and young Indian leaders indicate that Indians want to conserve all that is best in their own heritage as summed up in the slogan "Integrity, Not Integration." They say their tribal traditions give them a sense of identity, and in some tribes interest in teaching young children tribal dances and other traditions has reawakened. Indians say that in their own community setting identity is no problem. Problems arise when the Indian comes in contact with the "mainstream." Here the Indian has either no identity or a negative one.

Some observers believe that the expression "Chicano is Beautiful" is serving much the same purpose as "Black is Beautiful." Unlike Blacks, however, Mexican-Americans have fairly structured images of their past and have retained important elements of their heritage, including the language.

One manifestation of these minority group movements has been recent objections by the Blacks and Mexican-Americans that their children do not find themselves in the books produced in the United States. Until recently, authors of children's books, history books, comic strips, and television programs treated the black, brown, and red groups as though they did not exist, and when they appeared at all, only negative stereotypes were presented. Children have received practically no information about the culture, true nature, and contributions of these groups.

Within the past two or three years, however, tremendous changes have been occurring in all media. Many basal readers, such as Ginn's Reading 360 Program, now emphasize the plurality of United States culture. Trade books for children increasingly show black, brown, and red children and their families. Heroes and heroines of these groups are also appearing in children's books in increasing numbers. Some publishers now employ ethnic consultants to review manuscripts for inaccuracies and omissions of minority group contributions. In comic strips and cartoons, the Black child from the inner city can find himself portrayed with ethnic authenticity through *Luther* and *Wee Pals.* He can also see himself in TV productions such as *"Sesame Street."* *Luther* and *"Sesame Street"* are examples of mass media that deliberately try to help young Blacks in their search for healthy identities. It remains for social scientists, educators, writers for children, toy makers, and others to support the idea of racial pride with their creative productions and research.

Although some headway has been made in presenting minority

groups in the media, the picture remains bleak. Minorities are economically, religiously, and academically exploited. Much profit is realized annually by maintaining ghettos and exploiting American Indians on reservations. Religious groups pressure minorities to join their failing churches. Underclothed, underfed, poverty-stricken children often see themselves stereotyped as worthless. Here there is little opportunity for developing healthy identities. Although much money is spent each year to study poverty and minority culture, being studied immediately places one in an inferior position, at least as studies are usually conducted. While studies are profitable for some, they have become another means of cruel exploitation.

Even when the Federal Government grants money to ameliorate the effects of such abuses, further abuses occur and funds are often diverted from their intended purpose. As this report is being written, newspapers are recounting such abuses in Head Start programs in Harlem, in predominantly Indian schools, and in programs for Mexican-American children. One reader of the "confidential" report of the Harvard Center for Law and Education on the use of Federal funds intended for deprived Indian children writes that "every page of the document bristles with abuses." Funds intended for school lunches for Indians were often subverted, leaving Indian children with empty stomachs. Navajo parents were known to have sold their sheep and pawned their few possessions to pay the lunch bills sent home by school authorities. Transportation funds seemed to vanish as did funds to improve school buildings so inadequate as to constitute health hazards.

Paralleling the movements for more healthy racial and ethnic identities are movements designed to bring about more favorable and realistic identities for women. A major focus of these movements has been to create new identities for women with accompanying changes in the treatment of females from infancy through employment, career development, and old age. Like Blacks, the militant women's organizations are bringing about change in the history books, writing children's books that change the female stereotype, and writing books about the heroines of history.

For the emergence of strong, healthy identities, all children must interact with a healthy emotional and physical environment. Many children have healthy emotional environments in the early months of life when their universe is limited to their family. However, most children encounter hostile emotional, behavioral, and physical environments once their universe extends beyond the family unit or immediate neighborhood. Either they are not exposed to other cultures and races, a subtle form of racism, or they experience early destructive effects of overt racism.

In addition, community planning and design often serves the needs of industry, neglecting its most important citizens, children. Childhood has been regarded simply as a transitional period to adulthood, yet we always have children with us. Houses, public buildings, furniture, and recreational areas have been constructed (except for a token swing) for adult living, as if no children are expected to live "there."

With the current rates of urbanization, automation, pollution, and social and technological change, it is increasingly urgent to make the environment more favorable to the emergence of healthy identity among young children.

The fundamental goal of Forum 2 is to enable all children to develop healthy, strong identities during their early years, so they may have a chance to fully realize their potentialities. This goal can be attained only if the child's environment responds to his or her individuality (even before birth). The child should be taught from birth about his individuality, and the environment should recognize, acknowledge, and respect the child's individuality.

Since the child's identity and the environment's response to this identity serve as powerful guides to a child's behavior, failure to attain this goal will prevent children from reaching their full potential. The results will be increased rates of delinquency and crime, increasing rates of emotional disturbance and mental illness, debased talent, violence and destruction, and general lack of involvement in life and work. Conditions inimical to the emergence of strong, healthy identities among young children have reached a danger point which threatens to destroy our society.

The new agencies and measures proposed in the following section were those judged most promising for solving problems of sound identity emergence and achieving our goal.

Children, who are powerless and need a strong voice to represent them as a minority group, are now without political clout in this country. Therefore, *we recommend that top priority be given to quickly establishing a child advocacy agency financed by the Federal Government and other sources with full ethnic, cultural, racial, and sexual representation.* This agency would be highly autonomous and be charged with fostering, coordinating, and implementing all programs related to the emergence and development of healthy identity among children. The agency would be especially concerned with programs to strengthen family life in all its forms, including: education for parenting, which emphasizes and values the uniqueness of every child; establishing a national commission to strengthen and enhance cultural pluralism, developing community-based comprehensive resource centers for families; and establishing child-oriented environmental commissions at national, state, and local levels.

In view of our past neglect of children, Forum 2 believes that such an agency is necessary before other recommendations can be effectively implemented.

The following guidelines are suggested for implementing this recommendation:

- The system shall include a Child Advocate who is a member of the Cabinet of the President of the United States; an interdepartmental office directly under the President's office, headed by the Child Advocate, which coordinates all Federal agencies in matters related to children; a Child Advocate at the state level in every state who reports directly to the governor; a Child Advocate on every governing body of cities, towns, and villages.

- Funding at the national level shall be similar to that of the American Red Cross, which receives funds not only from the Federal Government but from other sources, public and private. A high level of autonomy in system operation and utilization of funds must be assured at all levels.

- The national Child Advocate's office would be under the control of a national policy board which would establish operating policies and priorities. A similar structure would operate at the state and local levels.

- The national policy committee would include representatives from the parent and youth categories, as well as representatives of cultural, ethnic, racial, and sex categories.

- The method of selecting the national policy committee must ensure that most members will not be political appointments of the national administration but will *primarily* include members selected in a democratic process so that members represent divergent interests and positions.

We recommend a new organizational form, such as a neighborhood resource and service center, to coordinate all community programs that can help families meet the needs of their children. Resources and services should be designed to eliminate those conditions that limit the nurture of a healthy sense of identity and the development of positive self-concepts. Such a center would have liaison with the local welfare department and make available public health, recreation, Veterans Administration, and other services [like] those provided by churches and private social agencies.

Neighborhood centers would be community controlled and locally autonomous. Services would be easily accessible and available to all on demand, on a 24-hour-a-day basis. The center would provide:

- Information and referral to all social services through a nationwide computer input system.
- Escort, transportation, and supportive relationships to enable individuals to use specialized services and resources not available within the center.
- One staff person as a citizen advocate with various bureaucratic systems.
- Training to develop indigenous resource personnel.

Comprehensive resources and services such as medical, dental, nutrition, psychological, public welfare, education, parent education, and training are essential for the feeling of well-being that generates and sustains one's sense of self-direction, dignity, and self-respect. These feelings and attitudes can be encouraged through programs that seriously consider social-emotional development curriculum, talent development activities, the development of family communication skills, and support for cultural diversity and identity. Deliberate efforts will be made to eliminate stereotypic racial, ethnic, and sexual roles in mass media, toys, and other program facilities.

The center's structure should be determined by the needs of the community served. A competent staff should be recruited and provisions made for career development of the indigenous members interested in this area of work. These personnel would represent all age levels, sexes, ethnic, and racial backgrounds.

Models from which these centers can be developed include: parent and child centers; comprehensive health centers; comprehensive mental health centers; new careers; neighborhood information centers; social services in Head Start; Lincoln Hospital, New York; Institute for Personal Effectiveness in Children, San Diego, California; Tom Gordon's Parent Effectiveness Training; Community Controlled Health Center, Cincinnati, Ohio; Institute for Training in Program Development, Los Angeles, California.

We recommend the establishment of a national commission to strengthen and enhance cultural pluralism within an independent child advocacy agency (or other appropriate agency). The charge of the commission would be: to strengthen, enhance, and make visible the pluralism that exists in our society; and to give tangible expression to the positive value of each individual's identity.

The goals of the commission are:

• To recognize the way each culture expresses itself through the arts and other outlets

• To utilize these diverse artistic forms and other expressions to strengthen each individual's identity and to bridge the existing gaps between different groups

• To protect the right of each individual and each group to maintain those differences that make ours a pluralistic society

• To create a climate in which social institutions assume a pluralistic character

• To take necessary steps to remove all oppressive actions of special interest groups, institutions, or governmental agencies which, for religious, political, or monetary gain, currently destroy or distort the identity of members of specific groups such as the American Indians.

The commission should include, on a policy-making level, professionals representing the wide spectrum of disciplines and individuals within our pluralistic society.

Selection of the commission will be the responsibility of the office of the Child Advocacy Agency (or other designated agency).

Suggested programs and services include:

- Supporting legislation on Federal, state, and local levels designed to further the purposes of the commission.
- Providing cultural exchange programs.
- Establishing and utilizing a "cultural voucher" system or "culture bank" on a national and regional basis.
- Providing short-term experiential programs, such as a children's exchange program, among children of varying backgrounds.
- Providing advisory and consultative services to mass media such as television, films, radio, and press to ensure a valid portrayal of any group within our society.
- Assisting individuals and groups seeking funds from private or governmental agencies for purposes related to the commission's goals. In achieving these purposes, the rights of persons or groups required to participate must not be violated.
- Providing the instruction and other resources required to develop and reward those kinds of giftedness valued by specific cultural groups.

We recommend that a multifaceted approach be used to convey information on human development and family relations to parents and parents-to-be and to others who interact with infants and young children.

Approaches should provide "how to" information and techniques for day-to-day child rearing, and should provide the parents understanding of how a child's healthy and functional identity emerges. The rights and responsibilities of parenthood must also be conveyed.

Providing, at different levels, courses in child development and family relations should be a primary goal. These educational courses should help individuals appreciate the development processes of children in ways which will aid more creatively both the child in his struggle for identity and those who assume parental roles, either full-time or part-time, in their key responsibility for strengthening a child's sense of identity.

Two key avenues to follow in implementing parenting education are schools and the mass media.

Required courses in human development and family relations should be made available for girls and boys in both junior and senior high school.

It is anachronistic to consider adhering to the traditional nine-month school year at any level, including elementary. By using existing facilities throughout the entire year, greater flexibility can be achieved in existing curricula, and new programs may be introduced and implemented. Federal monies must be available to develop appropriate curricula on human development and to develop methods for use in the courses and in training qualified teachers.

Consideration could be given to developing work-study programs involving individuals in human development courses and day care centers (child development centers).

Colleges should provide required courses in human development and family relations at the undergraduate level.

In-service training composed of a core of courses should be required for teachers preparing to teach human development and family relations in any of a variety of educational settings.

The following areas of adult education should be made available:

- In-service training for interested and concerned adults (teachers and/or parents) in human development and other related courses in early childhood education. Expectant parents might, for example, be encouraged to take advantage of existing programs in community hospitals and, in smaller communities, individual programs offered by community medical clinics.

- Teachers and teacher assistants in day care or nursery schools (public, private, church) must have opportunities to take courses in child development and family relations.

- Vocational education, using materials and concepts embodied in training programs for child development assistants, should be incorporated in curricula of vocational and community colleges to serve the needs of post high school students or older adults.

The prescribed training programs should be offered by qualified instructors and an appropriate number of credit hours must be awarded and recognized upon completion. And participants graduating as salaried assistants to various human development professionals will find employment in programs such as day care, nursery school, hospital playrooms, day activity centers for mentally retarded children, and kindergartens.

Optimal time, effort, and funds are essential for research and development of program content and format and subsequent televising of resulting programs. The goal of these programs would be effective communication with parents and parents-to-be on:

- Positive and unique aspects of our pluralistic society
- Constructive approaches for children handicapped by blindness, deafness, birth deformities, mental retardation, physical injury, and emotional disturbance
- Resources for aiding intellectually gifted and creative children and children with outstanding talent in music, visual arts, dramatics, writing, and the like
- The fact that human beings are remarkably similar in their basic concerns for the welfare of all children

Long-range funding of the parents' television workshop would be derived from government, business, industry, labor, and private foundations.

Creative spot announcements should inform the public about all agencies and services that have existing programs for children and families or about special events pertaining to particular topics, for example, pregnancy and nutrition, childbirth, breast feeding, and discipline.

The Office of Child Development (OCD) must effectively serve as a clearing house and/or evaluator of all publications pertaining to child development and family relations.

The OCD should recognize and utilize expertise in the scientific and commercial community on how to increase the public appeal and utilization of such publications. For example, Madison Avenue advertising strategies must be used to prepare and disseminate UNICEF-quality material.

The OCD must underwrite the production of an evaluative "Consumer's Report" that deals with all literature pertaining to human development.

The OCD must ensure that all literature given a high rating is valid and free from racial, cultural, and sexual prejudices.

We recommend that child-oriented environmental commissions be established at national, state, and local levels to ensure that chil-

dren's needs are not neglected by city planners, architects, building *contractors, and others who influence how homes and neighborhoods* *are constructed.*

Only recently has active concern been expressed about what might be called ecological child psychology. In his recent book, Barker pointed out that a common view among psychologists is that "the environment of behavior is a relatively unstructured, passive, probabilistic arena of objects and events upon which man behaves in accordance with the programming he carries about within himself." Barker, however, proposes that the environment be viewed as "highly structured, improbable arrangements of objects and events that coerce behavior in accordance with their own dynamic patterning." Barker and his associates have found that they can predict some aspects of a child's behavior more adequately from behavior settings (drug stores, playgrounds, classrooms) than from knowledge of the behavior tendencies of the particular child.

The child's environment consists of those things, events, and persons who help the child define, establish, and maintain his identity. Prominent among these influences are parental and other adult model figures, ethnic customs, and the special environment in which the child develops. As we strengthen the value and meaning of these things, events, and persons in the child's life, we strengthen his identity.

An optimum physical environment would allow the child to successfully manipuate his surroundings at any age and would also provide a variety of sensual experiences. Children, however, have little say in structuring their environments, and the world remains essentially adult-centered.

A child-oriented environmental commission, possibly a division of Health, Education and Welfare or a child advocacy agency financed by Federal and local funds, could be composed of parents, pediatricians, educators, engineers, architects, and builders; it could operate at a national, state, or local level. The commission would advise, help plan, inspect, and approve construction and renovation of homes, apartments, public buildings, parks, day care centers (child development centers), and streets to meet the needs of children. For example, before the construction of a new shopping center, the commission would be responsible for consulting and advising the architects, merchants, and financiers about incorporating into the actual design of the center physical surroundings that are more stimulating to children, such as innovative flooring material whose color and texture make it more interesting for children to walk on, small-scale furniture, low-level displays which are either "child proof" or may be touched by a child without being damaged. It would also advise merchants on using their stores as learning experiences for children. A shoe store, for example, may display various types of leather which children would be invited to touch and investigate.

To further expand or improve a child's environment:

We recommend organizing a children's cultural committee to help expand a child's environment to include parks, zoos, museums, libraries, and other facilities of the larger community. A directory listing all available child-oriented activities—parks, zoos, libraries, clubs, and municipal buildings—could be collated by local, civic, or religious groups, publicized by volunteer media and advertising, and distributed by municipal outlets and interested commercial patrons.

Community centers should provide a variety of materials for children to explore and enjoy. Existing, but unused, schools or buildings can become community warehouses supplied with mechanical devices, scrap wood, clay, paper, and wheels, obtained through donations. The center could be supervised by day care centers, parents, or youth organizations.

Public health clinics could conduct seminars in how families can best utilize space in terms of identity formation—stressing the importance of privacy to a child and the need for a child to have his own place, no matter how small. Public health nurses and agencies should make such information available to crowded city dwellers.

The traditional conception of the family fails to accommodate the many other family forms now being recognized; and also fails to recognize that many families change over time. Because family membership in whatever form is a major environmental influence on children, we support Forum 14 in urging that the variability of family forms be recognized, that a presidential commission investigate legislation for its effect on family form and its discrimination against family structure, that an institute be created to study variant family structure and to support programs for basic family needs.

The editors of home furnishing and building magazines should be encouraged to consider child development more carefully in presenting home construction or decorating ideas, such as giving attention to children's play and traffic patterns.

Information should be amassed and disseminated on how families can make the best use of their environmental resources, and the availability of free materials and recreational facilities should be made known. Special attention should be given to making available resources for developing outstanding or unusual talents of families, especially among families living in poverty.

The preservation of green areas, playgrounds, parks, and living space in city planning and in neighborhood projects should be encouraged.

A concern for, and interest in, the preservation of the ecology should be developed in both children and parents.

The recommendations which have evolved from this 1970 White House Conference on Children are but a beginning. From here it becomes the responsibility of the delegates and other Conference participants to help set into motion the implementation of these recommendations. Furthermore, the Conference staff should devote their energies to setting up the means by which this may be done.

Nor should the process stop here. As we continue to evaluate our efforts, each state organization should begin to think toward the next conference. If these state organizations are included in the preliminary planning, the next conference can be developed with much greater delegate participation and much greater articulation between the state organizations and the forum task force groups. The Conference itself can then become a tool for tying together these concerns and for actually setting up the structures by which they may be met. As we go from this Conference with our concerns for meeting the needs of children, let us begin *now* to think of 1980.

PARENT AND CHILD—
THE HAZARDS OF EQUALITY

Thomas J. Cottle

Young people's involvement with adult authority—it's an old theme
hammered to life almost daily in studies published on parents of
adolescents, hippies, dropouts, druggies, militants, and the rest. Recently some writers "on youth" have openly chastised parents for
failing to assume assertive roles with their children. Even some
psychiatrists now argue for parental toughness, perhaps as a reaction
to an oft-blamed emphasis on permissiveness.

Authority implies an inequality or what some prefer to call an
asymmetry between the old and the young. There is no even exchange
between generations, nor is there ever a possibility for it. Parents are

"Parent and Child—The Hazards of Equality." From Thomas J. Cottle,
Time's Children: Impressions of Youth (Boston: Little, Brown and Company,
1969). Copyright © 1969, 1971 by Thomas J. Cottle. Reprinted by permission
of the publisher. This article originally appeared in *Saturday Review*.

87

by definition not peers, and their concern does not imply that they become colleagues. Yet the asymmetric structure of authority is not all bad, although parents and children are more than a bit ambivalent about it. Longing for the taste of adolescence, parents in many instances overstep the bounds that the asymmetry purports to guard. In some cases their intrusions are nothing short of disastrous. For some young people, a quiet inner strength vanishes when their parents trespass on the property of time and destroy the very same asymmetry that they themselves once wished to destroy.

The theme of authority is complicated, therefore, because young and old alike wish to tamper with the time of generations but realize the potentially devastating results of such an escapade. The asymmetry implies restraints on behavior, and the young, being today so profoundly aware of all the facts of life, recognize these restraints as well as anyone. Generally, the young seem more open than ever before, just as social reality seems more translucent. Perhaps there are fewer secrets today than yesterday, and perhaps too, our society honors revelation more than confidential trust.

There is little doubt that young people extend, prolong, or simply react to their parents' demands, be they uttered or silently passed on. Erik Erikson, the American psychoanalyst, has said that one generation revives the repressions of the generation before it. But, equally important, adolescents have become brilliant readers of parental intentions, or adults generally—including parents, teachers, ministers, deans, and psychotherapists—have become predictable or transparent in their dealings with the young. High school students now portray the "shrink scene" with ease. They anticipate, with frightening accuracy, the words and moods of churlish school administrators. A fifteen-year-old Negro boy told me that he could not get help from his school guidance counselor: "I wouldn't say this to his face, but he doesn't like Negroes. He may not even know this, but we know it." I spoke to the counselor in question. The student had not only correctly interpreted the man's attitude—his impersonation of the man's behavior, right down to the speech pattern, was perfect.

All of this suggests that the cat of the authority relationship is out of the bag. The young understand and appreciate adult motivations, and, significantly, the sociological rationalizations for their actions in authority contexts. While they may protest against school principals and programs, they confess a sympathy for their elders' plight of being trapped in the policies of some greater bureaucratic establishment, "the system." They recognize a "sell-out" or "game player" a mile away, and a heady college freshman, if the matter concerns him at all, can differentiate between the authentic liberal and the institutional brand from the last row of a lecture hall. Their language simplifications, such as "smarts," "head," "cool," "cop-out," are illustrations of an almost social-scientific terminology, which functions in reducing complex action patterns to succinct and manageable levels. Their language shows, moreover, the swiftness and clarity with which they can first interpret and then act upon personal and institutional demands. (Most students know that their parents' social class is still the best predictor of their own school success, and that the poor, and particularly the poor blacks, cannot hope to compete even with the omnipresent mediocrity found among the advantaged. Hence, their understanding of local school competition and mobility channels is profound, although frequently disillusioning and uninspiring.)

Perhaps the best illustration of language reflecting social sophistication and the apparent translucency of social reality is the expression "psyche out." A college junior assured me: "It's so easy to know what the teacher wants, or what he'll ask on a test. They never change. Give 'em what they want. You make them happy and you win." Even modest Phi Beta Kappa students claim they have "psyched out" their teachers and have emerged superior merely because they are better game players. The fact remains that to "psyche out" something is to stay one slender step ahead even of expectation. It is the ability to perceive the expression on the face of the future.

While it is hard for young people to be duped by authority figures, it is easy to be damaged by them, an act so often occurring when the superordinate—the elder, the parent, the teacher—wants to equalize what must remain as that asymmetric relationship. Again, asymmetry refers to relationships wherein the commodities exchanged are of unequal and, therefore, incomparable content, and the behavior of one person is not a call or demand for identical behavior in the other. In its most fundamental form, asymmetry describes relationships in which one of the members represents unquestioned authority in a particular context; hence, it refers to interactions engaging parents and children, teachers and students, and doctors and patients.

Several years ago, while leading a self-analytic group, I was invited to a party given by the members. As it was early in the group's history, it seemed reasonable that an informal evening together might loosen up and simplify all relationships. I was tempted to go, but a wiser man suggested that I not go. The asymmetry, he urged, ultimately must be preserved by the person holding authority. I may have lost something by declining, but I probably protected a valuable tension in the leader-member relationship. Moreover, the symbolic nature of the refusal reaffirmed the asymmetry, or inequality, which some of us working in groups feel is essential, and which members often confess, in their way, is preferred. The leader (or father) must in some sense forever remain the leader, and while this angers many, particularly those in groups, "humanness" is in no way automatically precluded by such a philosophy.

More recently, members of a self-analytic group observed their leader's participation in a political demonstration. At the following meeting they spoke of him with a newly discovered reverence. How good that he shares the same values; that he shows the courage to speak out against administrations. But they spoke, too, of a disgust for their mothers wearing mini-skirts and parents generally who act like kids. Anna, a mature young woman, told of a feeling of nausea that came over her when her roommate's mother reviewed the college courses she, the mother, was attending. Upon returning to her dormitory, Anna made a long-distance phone call home and luxuriated in the relief that her own mother still was pursuing mother-type activities: luncheons, museum visits, and food budgets.

The ambivalence is evident. Young people want to attack authority, and this is probably the way it must be. But in matters of human dealings, although not in issues of strict ideology, authority is not to "come down" to the child's level, as parents once perceptively felt it necessary to kneel down, if only to attain a spatial equality of the generations. Authority is not to give in; it is to remain firm in its commitment to preserve the essential asymmetry and the indelible generational separation, even if this means being seen as a "square" or "straight arrow."

When a small child orders his parent out of his bedroom, he necessarily fears the enormity of the act. In a tearful rage, he can only pray that the parent will go no farther than the living room. Similarly, when members express the intense desire to kick out the leader of self-analytic groups (in symbolic re-enactment of the primal horde story perhaps), invariably they want to know would he really go and would he return.

There is, then, a primitive core, developing first in interactions with parents, that pleads for the overthrow of authority, yet simultaneously for the inability to do it by nature of the superordinate's strength in resisting. Parents simply cannot break down or retreat. They must prevail, and no one wants this more than the child. In terms of this infantile core that stays with us, parents are perfect, without problems, immortal. Relationships with them preclude both equality and peership. A college student said it this way: "No matter what I do in the face of authority, I end up a child. It happens even when I don't know the authority. Are we forever children to older persons?"

For children to out-achieve their parents, an event not uncommon among college students (let us not forget that women, too, are confronted with career aspirations and the ensuing competitions as much as men), means that they, the younger, must delicately initiate revisions in parental relationships so that the older generation will not interpret the younger's accomplishments as their own dismal and static ineptitude. What an incredible task it is for these young and talented students to return during Christmas and summer vacations to the rooms and persons of their childhood; to return where all of us know we cannot again return, then to battle the very essence of an unjust but immutable temporality.

Why is it that each of us believes in the development, even in the successes, of our surging expectations, but see only aging in our parents? Perhaps the eternal danger of the immediate future is that while it guarantees reports of our most present investments, it brings first our parents, then us, closer to some inexplicable end. But for the handful of "right nows," our youthful preoccupations make only our own movement in the life space visible. All the rest, parents and teachers included, remains unchanged, timeless: "It's like they've stood still. They bring me back to my childhood hang-ups. They know I've grown up; they know I'm at college, but they're used to me as I was when I was last there."

These last phenomena are so clearly not the sensations of regression. Although we all have fought back urges to feel once more, for even a bittersweet interval, the winds of childhood, returning must not be mistaken for regressing. On the contrary, returning is resuming. This is what is meant by bringing one back to childhood "hang-ups." It seems like regression, for only in our direct involvements does family time again move ahead. In our separation, that certain time stops, and the stillness augurs death. But the student returns and time jolts forward again, alive, just as the family itself becomes vitally alive, although now life becomes a bit more cumbersome.

The predicament confronting the child at these times is to help his parents resolve the problems that occur when the young out-achieve their elders. Variations in accomplishment must be reconciled in ways that legitimately reinforce parents' ultimate authority and special superiority. Regardless of their attainments, son and daughter want to remain in the child's role, at least in this one context. The parents know the child's task and, like the vaudeville joke, the child knows the parents know, and the parents know the child knows they know.

It is in interpersonal dilemmas and gestures of this sort, gestures made and carried out in such public yet at the same time secretive ways, that families reaffirm health. The gestures imply the mutual recognition and trust of which Professor Erikson has spoken so poetically and firmly. By these gestures the social and temporal gaps are preserved, sociologic and psychologic genes are somehow passed from one generation to the next, and one is, in Erikson's words, able "to see one's own life in continuous perspective both in retrospect and in prospect" (*Young Man Luther*). The division, made first by time, permits the evolution of the adult and sanctifies the appropriateness and truth of the confirmation and the bar mitzvah. For sociological reasons, the gap between generations stays open. But it is all right because distance need not be construed as distrust, nor separateness as desertion.

For two years, I saw Kathy, who is now thirteen, in a hospital therapy setting. Her language and psychological test performance indicated a possible psychotic diagnosis. She had a recurring dream, one that intrigued us both, that she was in a forest being chased by a large bear. Up on its hind legs, it pursued and often caught her. The dream had become so terrifying that to prevent the bear from appearing, Kathy had resorted to magical powers symbolized in ritualized bedtime behavior. How terribly symbolic was this content: the personification of impulses at the same time sexual and aggressive. How literal was the content: her father, an alcoholic for all of Kathy's life, returning home at night, pitifully drunk, staggering toward her, his shirt off, the hair on his chest plain and exposed, his smell, his pants open; pleading for sex at a locked bedroom door, being rejected by his wife until he promises to "grow up and behave like a man," masturbating as a little girl watches, bewildered and horrified.

Like Kathy, too many children have been freaked out by some form of family drama. Now, although nascent and unconscious, their strategy is to get out of their homes, out of their lives, and out of their minds. What a miracle it is that some stay, conjuring up reasons for the necessity of their remaining close. But the muffled aggression in their loyalty is unmistakable. The children and their parents are like the envied lovers in the old story who never stopped holding hands until just once, whereupon they beat each other to death. Holding on to a mother's skirt after all, may be more than a wish to remain near and in touch. It may be playing the boxer who by staying in a clinch, prevents himself and his opponent from manning battle stations at arm's length.

When a thoughtless and angry Cambridge mayor's purge on young people led him to chastise hippies for having run away from home, I reacted by thinking on the contrary. The parents must have run away first, in some fashion, hence the children merely followed suit. Now, after examining life stories I wonder whether, like the most domesticated of pets, "pre-hippies" ran because their parents rushed them and frightened them and got too close too soon. I wonder whether it was because they felt emotionally crowded by their parents that they "split." Still, even in unabandoned escape and angered protestation, children may be responding to or fulfilling some communicated need or directive. How curious is the thought, therefore, that protest and escape represent obeisance turned upside down.

It is equally curious that the familiar "need-to-escape-from-it-all" explanation of intoxication is used again when referring to serious drug-taking as a desire to repress. Mickey is a handsome, young high school dropout with an exceptional literary talent. When he was eleven, his parents fought so bitterly that he often found his mother lying in a pool of blood. Mickey would have to call for the ambulance and later on, after nursing his mother back to health, he would turn his attention to reuniting his parents.

During one cryptic account of a drug experience, he practically went into a swoon: "But when you come down, man, you come down hard, and that taking each moment one by one dissolves into that rotten other present, the one where you say, I gotta go back to my job. And you ask yourself, why do I do it, and you know, you gotta feel responsible. But it's OK because you think about the next high." I suggested to Mickey that coming down means having to think about tomorrow. "Wrong, man," he smiled for he had one on the shrink, "it's the past. It's on your back like you know what! . . . You say why did it have to happen to me?"

In speaking with Mickey and boys like him, one senses an ironical and twisted searching for insanity. Where the shocks of childhood were merely flirtations with craziness, by sixteen they have reappeared as an open willingness to consider "steady dating." At first only a couple of times a week; later on, every day and every night. The apparent psychotic quality or "way-outness" of the drugs is at once terrifying and exhilarating. The downs hurt but serve to affirm the lingering presence of sanity, or at least the ability to call upon it. If the user is sure it's still there, he goes back up on top again.

Not ironically, the very same strategy—"blowing the mind"—is used as a way of keeping out the mind-blowing experiences that might have urged persons toward this action in the first place. But just as drinking fails to induce forgetfulness, drugs seem to be failing many persons in their efforts to "repress" the past and keep it off their backs. If Timothy Leary is right, the next state will be electronic brain stimulation; hence, when pharmaceutical repression fails, attempts may be made at total memory ablation. At that time, a metaphysical present will evolve, free of any recollections and expectations, free of all regrets and despair.

Failing to understand so many of these complicated and gifted people, I often forget myself and remind them of their futures as parents. It is not that easy. For one thing, their very sense of future differs from mine. Moreover, the option to "start again" in marriage is highly problematic. Many fear they will repeat the desecrating scenes of their childhood: "I'll ruin my kid a helluva lot more than the drugs I take will"; "Are you kidding, man? Can you see me as a father? You gotta be nuts! And you a shrink!"; "A freak kid's gotta better chance than I did!"

If starting again were possible, most would probably opt for total recommencement. Knowing full well that their parents never wanted them in the first place, some almost cannot go back far enough to reach a time when their own histories might have started off on a good footing. No one admits it, however, for that would be to proclaim absolutely one's non-being. It would be to break the slim and delicate threads that now barely hold the generations pridefully together. Kathy told me that her mother was informed by doctors that she could have no more children after the birth of Kathy's nearest older sister. In fact, two more children were born. The mother admitted she had not wanted either one. Her "not wanting" became the daughter's description of herself as the "unexpected surprise." Kathy and I knew that she understood the conditions of her origin and the facts of her life. Indeed, I felt that her rather protracted inability to comprehend how children are born might have symbolized an even more profound reluctance and self-protection.

Regrettably, the concept of insanity pervades the worlds, however expansive, of many young people. What many want to know is utterly predictable: "Just tell me one thing, man; am I crazy? I mean, you know, am I crazy?" The word "crazy" is ubiquitous. It has lost its primeval jolt, but it holds on to an unmodifiable message. There is, however, plenty of insanity left over in television scripts and movies. Insanity is feared when witnessing the inexplicable behavior of those around us as they do nothing more than fight aggressively for social and private rights too long in coming. It is also feared when witnessing those well meaning men who seek to control those who protest. The young hear the President called mad and the war insane, and they puzzle over insanity's bewildering function in jury trials, and partly because of this they seek it as a way of getting out of the draft.

In my day, not so long ago, a "joking" admonition for guaranteed military deferment was, when the army doctor examines you, kiss him. Now it's insanity. Naturally, the worry exists that they might carry forever the brand of insanity on their sleeves just about where the private stripe might have gone. To be crazy is to avoid military service. Like kissing the doc, it is the avoidance of maleness. An often cruel society rubs this in: A real man fights for his country. Ideologies and spirit react against this, but the doubt stays. American socialization patterns, normally instituting strict sex-role differentiations, take care of that. There will be a lingering doubt, although in much of their questioning and concern, perceptions and anguish, the young are supported. Many of the "knowing class," they come to learn, now prefer to think of "business as usual" as the real insanity course, and jail as an undesirable but honorable way out.

Earlier I spoke of a resistance to bearing children and the feeling that one cannot successfully assume responsibilities of parenthood. In some cases it seems as though the diffidence displayed in "going on" masks a wish to start anew. The present urge to keep the cycle from repeating and the intention to keep fresh life from beginning must be considered from the point of view of sexuality. Although the language remains unchanged, industries of "procuring" and "scoring" today refer to drugs. The prophylactic, its slick package dirtied by months in the seams of an old wallet, has been replaced by the nickel bag: "Always be prepared." A funny reversal regards sex-role functions in a new economic market, as girls now solicit funds to pay for their boyfriends' stuff. I was stopped by one of these girls in the street on a beautiful October day: "Excuse me, Sir," she began her proposal. "How about a quarter for a cup of God knows what?"

One cannot be certain of the sexual habits of the persons of whom I speak. Anyway, it's no one's business until they mention it. The subject, however, is close to the conversational surface. It is as intimate as it ever was, but beginning to be freed of its irrational ties to some mysterious and primordial secrecy. As with much of their behavior, many of the young merely make overt what their elders do covertly. In so doing, they seem much more honest and far less foolish. However, the conspicuous consumption of other youngsters is little more than a mimicry of their parents.

Many young men on drugs confess their apprehensions about homosexuality. It is not simply that they fear their impulses; this seems more common among those actually engaged in heterosexual relationships. Instead, they tell of a lack of sexual impulses and a concern that perhaps drugs have destroyed the sex drive. Because of their sophistication, they comprehend the possibility that their activities generally could be interpreted as homosexual, but they manifest little panic about this. Some admit that they are able to "make it" with girls only when "high." They confess to fright, but it does not compare to the fear that they may be crazy.

This is the supreme danger, as it suggests again the complex reversal of not only competence in drug and sex work, but the associated interchange between the organs of sex and the "organ" of drugs, the mind. One almost wants to assert that a phallic phase of development has been temporarily supplanted or postponed by a "cephalic" phase. All life is fixated in the mind, and Leary spoke for the generation at least once when he advertised that each brain cell is capable of brilliant and repeating orgasms.

This then leaves one issue: the "freak-out," the ultimate reward —the ultimate punishment. It is total destruction, at once implosion and explosion. In their own words, it is brain damage and disintegration. It is, simultaneously, conception, pregnancy, childbirth, castration, and death. Some continue to believe that from the womb of the mind, a new child, a freak child is born.

By their own admission, the freak-out is also a premediated copout. Like living with a woman unmarried, it is anticipated endingness and the preparation for a later recourse. Demanding no commitment, it is an out, permitting the luxury of retiring as undefeated champion. No one can find fault with the last-minute term paper writer or the hospital patient. Both have their excuses. Both wonder, presumably, about what their competence might be like void of recourse. Both wonder, too, about the lack of preparation for the equivocal future and the minimal confidence displayed in present endeavor.

Depicted in most of these notions is the mass communicative society in which we survive. The accomplishments by so many are so great, the knowledge and awareness so swift in arrival and so deep in meaning, that in a way we leave the young no excuse for failure other than severe illness and total collapse. Adlai Stevenson once confessed relief that career decisions were behind him. It's hard to be young today, he observed. So many good people are already so advanced in practically any area that one might choose for himself. Perhaps this is the reason why some drop out.

In sexual relations, the excuse that probably maintained the sanity of frightened generations of men no longer exists. Girls have "the pill," and aggressive action now swings both ways. Students offer apologies for not smoking pot and agonize over an inability to get excited, much less involved, in political enterprises. To be straight is to be square, and like it or not, the straight become defensive and tempted.

Our televised and instant-replay society also allows fewer secrets. We see the war; we see men murdered; and we become frustrated when we cannot discover the exact frame on which is recorded a President's death. Our newspapers pry and our movies reveal, and so too, apparently, do some parents. Where many children fantasize that the secrets they guard preserve some mysterious family integrity, others, in fact, are maintaining this integrity by biting a quivering lip in fear that exposure of their treasured secrets will cause their families to unravel. All the while, performance-demands shriek for attention. One must compete and succeed often enough; make it on his own; and react to the war and the fact that he or a boyfriend will soon be drafted and, not so unlikely, killed! One must be good in school, good at home, good at sports, good at pot, and good in bed. Life becomes unmanageably meaningful. It is enough to make one (want to) go insane.

Most make it, however, even with the knowledge that their culture warns of belligerent Chinese, overkill, and an equivocal future. One cannot know when the next and final war will come, or when past experience with drugs will suddenly re-erupt in the form of a grotesque child or one's own psychotic demise. Unmistakably near, death becomes a real reality. Less fuzzy than ever before, its shape and sound hover about self-analytic groups, bull sessions, and coffee dates. Damn the future and the inevitable! It was better in the Thirties when gravelly throated heroes sang into megaphones. It was better, too, in the last century when men wore frock coats, beards, and long hair. It was better and easier because it was the past, and perception of the completed proves the validity of survival, if not achievement. At the very least, the past means having got this far. It also means the seat of much of the trouble.

Some young people reveal a peculiar attitude about the past. It is not merely a time that was, but the series of events that once were, yet somehow continue to remain as the present's lining. Neither recalled nor retrieved, the past has become the stuff of moment-to-moment encounter and the routine of day work. The past has not yet become past in the sense of being over, because its foundation, like a child's body, remains soft and unfinished. There are no completions, no triumphs, no guaranteed deferrals or subsistence.

No one as yet has studied the notes written by parents to their runaway children in New York's East Village or San Francisco's Haight-Ashbury district. These pitiful missives document so well the lack of generational space and the confession of failure in parenthood and adulthood. They could be the letters of children, who, wishing to come home, promise never again to misbehave. If they did not cause guilt or confusion in the recepients, hippies would have little need to prevent them from reaching the runaway child. (Those people whose self-appointed task is to maintain the separation and lack of communication between parent and child must fear the fruits of love's temptation, the very philosophy they profess. Moreover, they are reminiscent of professional mourners, who periodically remind the congregation or family of the recent loss by crying when others attain momentary composure.)

The "come back home; all is forgiven" notes stand as a testament to what must be seen by the young as a crumbling structure, or a tragic reversal of intentionality and interpersonal competence. They reflect adult pleas for help and forgiveness, and as such they represent a far worse social fact than hippie farm colonies or pot parties. The notes only document what the poets know so well: Of all rewards, youth is a supreme ideal. The old wish to be young, and the young are happy exactly where they are.

Few parents are able to accept the passing of adolescence, especially when their own children dramatize more vibrantly than ever the former gratifications and projected incompleteness of their own lives. It is inconceivable to think that young people have ever been simultaneously idolized and despised, worshiped and envied as they are presently. Without doubt, the problem of age-grading is now of paramount significance in the United States. It is *the* dimension: Good or bad, the old are preoccupied with the young, and the young are preoccupied with themselves.

When the activities of the young were secretive, adults were compelled to deal with their own imaginations. Now, when sexuality, in particular, screams at us from advertisements, fashions, television, movies, and magazines, it becomes increasingly difficult to decline youth's unintended invitation and accept the process and reality of aging. Adults must work hard to avoid the eternal seductions of the young, for these affairs simply do not work out. Time inevitably chaperones such liaisons, and the primordial strain that comes about through the separation of generations never will permit a successful consummation of these two hearts, the young and old.

The seduction does not stop with parents, however, for the succulence of youth is dreamed of each day by teachers, counselors, therapists, ministers, etc. A most dangerous tack for any of these persons is to be uncritically won over by youth's stated demands and ideologies or interpretations of them. An example of this point seems in order. We are emerging from an unfortunate era in which psychotherapy was viewed as either panacea or black magic. Psychotherapists finally have undertaken critical self-scrutinization and for the most part, attacks on theory and procedure have resulted in clarifying statements for the practitioners. Still, there are some critics who expend a suspiciously great amount of energy communicating to youth the evils of psychotherapy and even more benign adult interventions. By acting this way, they signify their "stand with youth," a stand normally introduced by some phrase which seems an apologia, but which in truth is more a boastful pledge to be young like the young.

Frequently, these critics demonstrate a striking accuracy in their realignment of youth's goals, ambitions, and philosophies. Just as often, their arguments are indecorous and evil. Many young people, in fact, do find illness in themselves and do seek help. They despise the proverbial "shrink scene" and rightly so, but in their quest of a "hip shrink," they wish for a modification—or, better, modernization—of the psychotherapeutic relationship, but not its annihilation. They know it is no panacea, but in anticipation they feel it has worth and are willing to try. The best adults can do, therefore, is to experiment with the helping apparatus and not discourage the trying.

Those who aspire to speak for or understand youth must be aware of the seductive nature of their interests so that they will not reach the point where speaking for youth means no longer needing to listen to it. Genuine representation, after all, does not require reliving; it requires recalling.

One final point regards the heightened sophistication of the young, their eagerness to speak, their access to recesses of an experienced childhood, and their poignant observations of adulthood. While each generation can expect to live longer, much of society, as Erikson points out, demands that individuals be allotted less time for youth.

Earnest young proto-professionals especially uphold this ethic. Scattered not so infrequently about, however, are those whose parents have denied them even this minuscule tenure. For most, the awareness is simply a function of a precocious curiosity and creative need to experience. For the ones knowingly in trouble, the most immediate and pressing action resembles an attempt to complete some poorly understood mission started long ago by someone else.

That time repeats itself is but a comforting saying. The concept of a family cycle, moreover, is misleading as it tends to slur over the individual cycles unwinding at various tempi within it. Individual cycles never repeat themselves, for in progressing or carrying on in any guise, healthy or sick, the young, as ingenious as they are, do little more than obey the wishes of others and the demands that time imposes. Typically, the directions given by those who were here before us are to wait patiently and not walk so fast.

Sociologists have written that a major function of social structures is to direct its members to appropriate goal states, means of attaining them, and attitudes that may be taken in evaluating goals and means. The desire to become a doctor or lawyer, indeed the need to achieve, does not come from out of the blue. These are learned. So too is the desire to rebel, have sex, take drugs, escape, and even "freak out." In their way, all of these actions are creative because they develop out of social forms of, as well as private needs for, expression. But they have not "sprung up"; like instincts, they have evolved.

For many today, the evolution is not satisfying, and the internal excursions and elaborations have become (and probably started out as), in David Riesman's terms, "other-directed" movements. Knowing exactly this, many young persons continue, nonetheless, in their other-directed patterns, and thereby show themselves most willing to listen outward and upward. Considering much of our adult behavior, this fact is remarkable.

DELINQUENTS WITHOUT CRIME

Paul Lerman

About 100 years ago, the state of New Jersey built a special correctional facility to save wayward girls from a life of crime and immorality. Over the years the ethnic and racial backgrounds of the institutionalized girls changed, the educational level of their cottage parent-custodians shifted upward, and the program of correction grew more humane. But the types of offenses that constitute the legal justification for their incarceration in the State Home for Girls have not changed, not appreciably.

The vast majority of the girls in the Home today, as in past years, were accused of misbehavior that would not be considered crimes if committed by adults. They were formally adjudicated and

"Delinquents without Crime," by Paul Lerman. (Originally titled "Child Convicts.") From *Transaction*, Vol. 8 (July/August 1971). © 1971 by Transaction, Inc. Reprinted by permission of the author and the publisher.

institutionalized as delinquents, but most of them have not committed real criminal acts. Over 80 percent of them in 1969 were institutionalized for the following misdeeds: running away from home, being incorrigible, ungovernable and beyond the control of parents, being truant, engaging in sexual relations, and becoming pregnant. Criminologists classify this mixture of noncriminal acts "juvenile status offenses," since only persons of a juvenile status can be accused, convicted and sentenced as delinquents for committing them. Juvenile status offenses apply to boys as well as girls, and they form the bases for juvenile court proceedings in all 50 states.

Most Americans are probably unaware that juveniles are subject to stricter laws than adults, and to more severe penalties for noncriminal acts than are many adults who commit felonies. This practice, so apparently antithetical to our national conceit of child-centeredness, began well before the Revolution. The Puritans of the Plymouth Bay Colony initiated the practice of defining and treating as criminal children who were "rude, stubborn, and unruly," or who behaved "disobediently and disorderly towards their parents, masters, and governors." In 1824, when the House of Refuge established the first American juvenile correctional institution in New York City, the Board of Managers was granted explicit sanction by the state legislature to hold in custody and correct youths who were leading a "vicious or vagrant life," as well as those convicted of any crime. The first juvenile court statute, passed in Illinois in 1899, continued the tradition of treating juvenile status offenses as criminal by including this class of actions as part of the definition of "delinquency." Other states copied this legislative practice as they boarded the bandwagon of court reform.

My contention that juvenile status offenders are still handled through a *criminal* process will be disputed by many defenders of the current system who argue that the creation of the juvenile court marked a significant break with the past. They contend that juvenile courts were set up to deal with the child and his needs, rather than with his offense. In line with this benign aim, the offense was to be viewed as a symptom of a child's need for special assistance. The juvenile court was designed to save children—not punish them. Only "neglectful" parents were deemed appropriate targets of punishment.

Unfortunately, the laudable intentions of the founders of the court movement have yet to be translated into reality. The United

States Supreme Court, in 1967, reached this conclusion; so, too, did the Task Force on Delinquency of the President's Commission on Law Enforcement and the Administration of Justice. Both governmental bodies ruled that juvenile court dispositions were, in effect, sentences that bore a remarkable resemblance to the outcomes of adult criminal proceedings. The Supreme Court was appalled at the idea that 15-year-old Gerald Gault could be deprived of his liberty for up to six years without the benefits of due process of law found in adult courts. The majority was persuaded that the consequences of judicial decisions should be considered, not just the ideals of the founders of the juvenile court.

Since the Supreme Court ruling in *Gault v. Arizona,* there has been increased concern and debate over the introduction of legal counsel and minimal procedural rights in the operation of the juvenile court. The preoccupaton with legal rights in the courtroom has, however, obscured the fact that the sociolegal boundaries of delinquency statutes were unaffected by *Gault.* Nevertheless, some revision of the laws has been undertaken by the states, at least since 1960 when the Second United Nations Congress on the Prevention of Crime and the Treatment of Offenders recommended that juveniles should not be prosecuted as delinquents for behavior which, if exhibited by adults, would not be a matter of legal concern.

One state, New York, even approached a technical compliance with the United Nations standard. In New York, juvenile status offenders are adjudicated with a separate petition alleging a "person in need of supervision" (PINS); traditional criminal offenses use a petition that alleges "delinquency." However, true to American tradition, both types of petitioned young people are locked up in the same detention facilities and reform schools. One of the most "progressive" juvenile court laws in the country was initially enacted with restrictions on mixing, but this was soon amended to permit the change to be merely semantic, not substantive. Besides New York, six other states have amended their juvenile codes to establish a distinctive labeling procedure to distinguish criminal and noncriminal acts. Each of these states (California, Illinois, Kansas, Colorado, Oklahoma and Vermont) has banned *initial* commitment to juvenile reformatories of children within the noncriminal jurisdiction of the court. Whether this ban will be continued in practice (and in the statutes) is uncertain. Meanwhile, young people can still be mixed in detention facilities, transfers to reformatories are technically possible, and subsequent commitments to delinquent institutions are apparently permitted. In addition, it is doubtful whether the public (including teachers and prospective employers) distinguishes between those "in need of supervision" and delinquents.

THE POLICE AS DUTCH UNCLES

If the letter and spirit of American juvenile statutes were rigorously enforced, our delinquency rates and facilities would be in even deeper trouble than they are today. For few American youth would reach adulthood without being liable to its stern proscriptions. However, mitigating devices are used to avoid further overcrowding court dockets and institutions, and to demonstrate that parents and enforcement officials can be humane and child-centered. Adult authorities are permitted to exercise discretionary behavior in processing actions by official petitions. The American system is notorious for its widespread use of unofficial police and judicial recording and supervision of juveniles, whether status offenders or real delinquents. As a matter of historical fact, the hallmark of the American system is the intriguing combination of limitless scope of our delinquency statutes and enormous discretion granted in their enforcement and administration. Our statutes appear to reflect the image of the stern Puritan father, but our officials are permitted to behave like Dutch uncles—if they are so inclined.

Discretionary decision making by law enforcement officials has often been justified on the grounds that it permits an "individualization" of offenders, as well as for reasons of pragmatic efficiency. While this may be true in some cases, it is difficult to read the historical record and not conclude that many juvenile status actions could have been defined as cultural differences and childhood play fads, as well as childhood troubles with home, school and sex. Using the same broad definition of delinquency, reasonable adults have differed—and continue to differ—over the sociolegal meaning of profanity, smoking, drinking, sexual congress, exploring abandoned buildings, playing in forbidden places, idling, hitching rides on buses, trucks and cars, sneaking into shows and subways and so forth. While many judgments about the seriousness of these offenses may appear to be based on the merits of the individual case, delinquency definitions, in practice, employ shifting cultural standards to distinguish between childhood troubles, play fads and neighborhood differences. Today, officials in many communities appear more tolerant of profanity and smoking than those of the 1920s, but there is continuing concern regarding female sexuality, male braggadocio and disrespect of adult authority. In brief, whether or not a youth is defined as delinquent may depend on the era, community and ethnic status of the official—as well as the moral guidelines of individual law enforcers.

National studies of the prevalence of the problem are not readily available. However, we can piece together data that indicate that the problem is not inconsequential. A conservative estimate, based upon analysis of national juvenile court statistics compiled by the United States Children's Bureau, indicates that juvenile status crimes comprise about 25 percent of the children's cases initially appearing before juvenile courts on a formal petition. About one out of every five boys' delinquency petitions and over one-half of all girls' cases are based on charges for which an adult would not be legally liable ever to appear in court.

The formal petitions have an impact on the composition of juvenile facilities, as indicated by the outcomes of legal processing. A review of state and local detention facilities disclosed that 40 to 50 percent of the cases in custody, pending dispositional hearings by judges, consisted of delinquents who had committed no crimes. A study of nearly 20 correctional institutions in various parts of the country revealed that between 25 and 30 percent of their resident delinquent population consisted of young people convicted of a juvenile status offense.

The figures cited do not, however, reveal the number of youths that are treated informally by the police and the courts. Many young people are released with their cases recorded as "station adjustments"; in a similar fashion, thousands of youths are informally dealt with at court intake or at an unofficial court hearing. Even though these cases are not formally adjudicated, unofficial records are maintained and can be used against the children if they have any future run-ins with the police or courts. The number of these official, but nonadjudicated, contacts is difficult to estimate, since our requirements for social bookkeeping are far less stringent than our demands for financial accountability.

One careful study of police contacts in a middle-sized city, cited approvingly by a task force of the President's Commission on Law Enforcement and the Administration of Justice, disclosed that the offense that ranked highest as a delinquent act was "incorrigible, runaway"; "disorderly conduct" was second; "contact suspicion, investigation, and information" ranked third; and "theft" was a poor fourth. In addition to revealing that the police spend a disproportionate amount of their time attending to noncriminal offenses, the study also provides evidence that the problem is most acute in low-income areas of the city. This kind of finding could probably be duplicated in any city—large, small or middle-sized—in the United States.

LEGAL TREATMENT OF DELINQUENTS WITHOUT CRIMES

A useful way of furthering our understanding of the American approach to dealing with delinquents without crimes is provided by comparing judicial decisions for different types of offenses. This can be done by reanalyzing recent data reported by the Children's Bureau, classifying offenses according to their degree of seriousness. If we use standard FBI terminology, the most serious crimes can be labeled "Part I" and are: homicide, forcible rape, armed robbery, burglary, aggravated assault and theft of more than $50. All other offenses that would be crimes if committed by an adult, but are less serious, can be termed "all other adult types" and labeled "Part II." The third type of offenses, the least serious, are those acts that are "juvenile status offenses." By using these classifications, data reported to the Children's Bureau by the largest cities are reanalyzed to provide the information depicted in the table. Three types of decisions are compared in this analysis: 1) whether or not an official petition is drawn after a complaint has been made; 2) whether or not the juvenile is found guilty, if brought before the court on an official petition; and 3) whether or not the offender is placed or committed to an institution, if convicted. The rates for each decision level are computed for each of the offense classifications.

The table discloses a wide difference between offense classifications at the stage of deciding whether to draw up an official petition (57 percent versus 33 percent and 42 percent). Part I youth are far more likely to be brought into court on a petition, but juvenile status

DISPOSITION OF JUVENILE CASES AT THREE STAGES IN THE
JUDICIAL PROCESS, 19 OF THE 30 LARGEST CITIES, 1965

	PART I (MOST SERIOUS ADULT OFFENSES)	PART II (ALL OTHER ADULT OFFENSES)	JUVENILE STATUS OFFENSES
% Court Petition after complaint	57% N = (37,420)	33% (52,862)	42% (33,046)
% Convicted—if brought into court	92% N = (21,386)	90% (17,319)	94% (13,857)
% Placed or Committed— if convicted	23% N = (19,667)	18% (15,524)	26% (12,989)

offenders are processed at a higher rate than all other adult types. At
the conviction stage the differences are small, but the juvenile status
offenders are found guilty more often. At the critical decision point,
commitment to an institution, the least serious offenders are more
likely to be sent away than are the two other types.

It is apparent that juvenile justice in America's large cities can
mete out harsher dispositions for youth who have committed no
crimes than for those who violate criminal statutes. Once the petitions
are drawn up, juvenile judges appear to function as if degree of seriousness is not an important criterion of judicial decision making. If
different types of offenders were sent to different types of institutions,
it might be argued that the types of sentences actually varied. In fact,
however, all three offender types are generally sent to the same institutions in a particular state—according to their age and sex—for
an indeterminate length of time.

LENGTH OF INSTITUTIONALIZATION

If American juvenile courts do not follow one of the basic components of justice—matching the degree of punishment with the degree of social harm—perhaps the correctional institutions themselves
function differently. This outcome is unlikely, however, since the criteria for leaving institutions are not based on the nature of the offense.
Length of stay is more likely to be determined by the adjustment to
institutional rules and routine, the receptivity of parents or guardians
to receiving the children back home, available bed space in cottages
and the current treatment ideology. Juvenile status offenders tend to

have more family troubles and may actually have greater difficulty in meeting the criteria for release than their delinquent peers. The result is that the delinquents without crimes probably spend more time in institutions designed for delinquent youth than "real" delinquents. Empirical support for this conclusion emerges from a special study of one juvenile jurisdiction, the Manhattan borough of New York City. In a pilot study that focused on a random sample of officially adjudicated male cases appearing in Manhattan Court in 1963, I gathered data on the range, median and average length of stay for boys sent to institutions. In New York, as noted earlier, juvenile status youth are called "PINS" (persons in need of supervision), so I use this classification in comparing this length of institutionalization with that of "delinquents."

The range of institutional stay was two to 28 months for delinquents and four to 48 months for PINS boys; the median was nine months for delinquents and 13 months for PINS; and the average length of stay was 10.7 months for delinquents and 16.3 months for PINS. Regardless of the mode of measurement, it is apparent that institutionalization was proportionately longer for boys convicted and sentenced for juvenile status offenses than for juveniles convicted for criminal-type offenses.

These results on length of stay do not include the detention period, the stage of correctional processing prior to placement in an institution. Analyses of recent detention figures for all five boroughs of New York City revealed the following patterns: 1) PINS boys and girls are more likely to be detained than are delinquents (54 to 31 percent); and 2) once PINS youth are detained they are twice as likely to be detained for more than 30 days than are regular delinquents (50 to 25 percent). It is apparent that juvenile status offenders who receive the special label of "persons in need of supervision" tend to spend more time in custodial facilities at *all* stages of their correctional experience than do delinquents.

SOCIAL CHARACTERISTICS OF OFFENSES AND OFFENDERS

The offenses that delinquents without crimes are charged with do not involve a clear victim, as is the case in classical crimes of theft, robbery, burglary and assault. Rather, they involve young people who are themselves liable to be victimized for having childhood troubles or growing up differently. Three major categories appear to be of primary concern: behavior at home, behavior at school and sexual experimentation. "Running away," "incorrigibility," "ungovernability" and "beyond the control of parental supervision" refer to troubles with parents, guardians or relatives. "Growing up in idleness," "truanting" and creating "disturbances" in classrooms refer to troubles with teachers, principals, guidance counselors and school routines. Sexual relations as "minors" and out-of-wedlock pregnancy reflect adult concern with the act and consequences of precocious sexual experimentation. In brief, juvenile status offenses primarily encompass the problems of growing up.

Certain young people in American society are more likely to have these types of troubles with adults: girls, poor youth, rural migrants to the city, underachievers and the less sophisticated. Historically, as well as today, a community's more disadvantaged children are most likely to have their troubles defined as "delinquent." In the 1830s the sons and daughters of Irish immigrants were overrepresented in the House of Refuge, the nation's first juvenile correctional institution. In 1971 the sons and daughters of black slum dwellers [were] disproportionately dealt with as delinquents for experiencing problems in "growing up."

Unlike regular delinquents, juvenile status offenders often find a parent, guardian, relative or teacher as the chief complainant in court. Since juvenile courts have traditionally employed family functioning and stability as primary considerations in rendering dispositions, poor youth with troubles are at a distinct disadvantage compared to their delinquent peers. Mothers and fathers rarely bring their children to courts for robbing or assaulting nonfamily members; however, if their own authority is challenged, many parents are willing to use the power of the state to correct their offspring. In effect, many poor and powerless parents cooperate with the state to stigmatize and punish their children for having problems in growing up.

At least since *Gault,* the system of juvenile justice has been undergoing sharp attacks by legal and social critics. Many of these have pertinence for the processing and handling of juvenile status offenders. The current system has been criticized for the following reasons:

- The broad scope of delinquency statutes and juvenile court jurisdictions has permitted the coercive imposition of middle-class standards of child rearing.

- A broad definition has enlarged the limits of discretionary authority so that virtually any child can be deemed a delinquent if officials are persuaded that he needs correction.

- The presence of juvenile status offenses, as part of the delinquency statutes, provides an easier basis for convicting and incarcerating young people because it is difficult to defend against the vagueness of terms like "incorrigible" and "ungovernable."

- The mixing together of delinquents without crimes and real delinquents in detention centers and reform schools helps to provide learning experiences for the nondelinquents on how to become real delinquents.

- The public is generally unaware of the differences between "persons in need of supervision" and youths who rob, steal and assault, and thereby is not sensitized to the special needs of status offenders.

- Statistics on delinquency are misleading because we are usually unable to differentiate how much of the volume reflects greater public and official concern regarding home, school and sex problems, and how much is actual criminal conduct by juveniles.

- Juvenile status offenses do not constitute examples of social harm and, therefore, should not even be the subject of criminal-type sanctions.

- Juvenile institutions that house noncriminal offenders constitute the state's human garbage dump for taking care of all kinds of problem children, especially the poor.

- Most policemen and judges who make critical decisions about children's troubles are ill equipped to understand their problems or make sound judgments on their behalf.

- The current correctional system does not rehabilitate these youths and is therefore a questionable approach.

TWO UNINTENDED CONSEQUENCES

The Supreme Court in *Gault* found that the juvenile court of Arizona—and by implication the great majority of courts—was procedurally unfair. The court explicitly ruled out any consideration of the substantive issues of detention and incarceration. It may have chosen to do so because it sincerely believed that the soundest approach to ensuring substantive justice is making certain that juveniles are granted the constitutional safeguards of due process: the right to confront accusers and cross-examine, the right to counsel, the right to written charges and prior notice and the right against self-incrimination. Nevertheless, the inclusion of juvenile status offenders as liable to arrest, prosecution, detention and incarceration probably promotes the criminalization of disadvantaged youth. Earlier critics have indicated that incorrigible boys and girls sent to reform schools learn how to behave as homosexuals, thieves, drug users and burglars. But what is the impact at the community level, where young people initially learn the operational meaning of delinquency? From the child's point of view, he learns that occurrences that may be part of his daily life—squabbles at home, truancy and sexual precocity—are just as delinquent as thieving, robbing and assaulting. It must appear that nearly anyone he or she hangs around with is not only a "bad" kid but a delinquent one as well. In fact, there are studies that yield evidence that three-quarters of a generation of slum youth, ages ten to 17, have been officially noted as "delinquent" in a police or court file. It seems reasonable to infer that many of these records contain official legal definitions of essentially noncriminal acts that are done in the family, at school and with peers of the opposite sex.

It would be strange indeed if youth did not define themselves as "bad cats"—just as the officials undoubtedly do. It would be strange, too, if both the officials and the young people (and a segment of their parents) did not build on these invidious definitions by expecting further acts of "delinquency." As children grow older, they engage in a more consistent portrayal of their projected identity—and the officials dutifully record further notations to an expected social history of delinquency. What the officials prophesy is fulfilled in a process that criminalizes the young and justifies the prior actions of the official gatekeepers of the traditional system. Our social responses unwittingly compound the problem we ostensibly desire to prevent and control—real delinquent behavior.

In the arena of social affairs it appears that negative consequences are more likely to occur when there is a large gap in status, power and resources between the "savers" and those to be "saved." Evidently, colonial-type relationships, cultural misunderstandings and unrestrained coercion can often exacerbate problems, despite the best of intentions. Given this state of affairs, it appears likely that continual coercive intrusion by the state into the lives of youthful ghetto residents can continue to backfire on a large scale.

We have probably been componding our juvenile problem ever since 1824 when the New York State Legislature granted the Board of Managers of the House of Refuge broad discretionary authority to intervene coercively in the lives of youth until they become 21 years of age—even if they had not committed any criminal acts. Generations of reformers, professionals and academics have been too eager to praise the philanthropic and rehabilitative intentions of our treatment centers toward poor kids in trouble—and insufficiently sensitive to the actual consequences of an unjust system that aids and abets the criminalization of youth.

Sophisticated defenders of the traditional system are aware of many of these criticisms. They argue that the intent of all efforts in the juvenile field is to help, not to punish, the child. To extend this help they are prepared to use the authority of the state to coerce children who might otherwise be unwilling to make use of existing agencies. Not all acts of juvenile misbehavior that we currently label "status offenses" are attributable to cultural differences. Many youngsters do, in fact, experience troubles in growing up that should be of concern to a humane society. The fundamental issue revolves on how that concern can be expressed so as to yield the maximum social benefits and the minimum social costs. Thus, while the consequences of criminalizing the young and perpetuating an unjust system of juvenile justice should be accorded greater recognition than benign intentions, it would be a serious mistake to propose an alternative policy that did not incorporate a legitimate concern for the welfare of children.

NEW POLICY PERSPECTIVES

The issue is worth posing in this fashion because of a recent policy proposal advanced by the President's Commission on Law Enforcement and the Administration of Justice. The commission suggested that "serious consideration should be given complete elimination from the court's jurisdiction of conduct illegal only for a child. Abandoning the possibility of coercive power over a child who is acting in a seriously self-destructive way would mean losing the opportunity of reclamation in a few cases."

Changing delinquency statutes and the jurisdictional scope of the juvenile court to exclude conduct illegal only for a child would certainly be a useful beginning. However, the evidence suggests that the cases of serious self-destructiveness are not "few" in number, and there is reason to believe that many adjudicated and institutionalized young people do require some assistance from a concerned society. By failing to suggest additional policy guidelines for providing the necessary services in a *civil* context, the commission advanced only half a policy and provided only a limited sense of historical perspective.

Traditional American practices toward children in trouble have not been amiss because of our humanitarian concern, but because we coupled this concern with the continuation of prior practices whereby disliked behavior was defined and treated as a criminal offense (that is, delinquent). Unfortunately, our concern has often been linked to the coercive authority of the police powers of the state. The problems of homeless and runaway youths, truants, sex experimenters and others with childhood troubles could have been more consistently defined as *child welfare* problems. Many private agencies did emerge to take care of such children, but they inevitably left the more difficult cases for the state to service as "delinquents." In addition, the private sector never provided the services to match the concern that underlay the excessive demand. The problem of the troublesome juvenile status offender has been inextricably linked to: 1) our failure to broaden governmental responsibility to take care of *all* child welfare problems that were not being cared for by private social agencies; and 2) our failure to hold private agencies accountable for those they did serve with public subsidies. We permitted the police, courts and correctional institutions to function as our residual agency for caring for children in trouble. Many state correctional agencies have become, unwittingly, modern versions of a poorhouse for juveniles. Our *systems* of child welfare and juvenile justice, *not* just our legal codes, are faulty.

The elimination of juvenile status offenses from the jurisdiction of the juvenile court would probably create an anomalous situation in juvenile jurisprudence if dependency and neglect cases were not also removed. It would be ironic if we left two categories that were clearly noncriminal within a delinquency adjudicatory structure. If they were removed, as they should be, then the juvenile court would be streamlined to deal with a primary function: the just adjudication and disposition of young people alleged to have committed acts that would be criminal if enacted by an adult. Adherence to this limited jurisdiction would aid the court in complying with recent Supreme Court rulings, for adversary proceedings are least suited to problems involving family and childhood troubles.

If these three categories were removed from the traditional system, we would have to evolve a way of thinking about a new public organization that would engage in a variety of functions: fact finding, hearing of complaints, regulatory dispositions and provision of general child care and family services. This new public agency could be empowered to combine many of the existing functions of the court and child welfare departments, with one major prohibition: transfers of temporary custody of children would have to be voluntary on the part of parents, and all contested cases would have to be adjudicated by a civil court. This prohibition would be in harmony with the modern child welfare view of keeping natural families intact, and acting otherwise only when all remedial efforts have clearly failed.

We have regulatory commissions in many areas of social concern in America, thereby sidestepping the usual judicial structure. If there is a legitimate concern in the area of child and family welfare, and society wants to ensure the maintenance of minimum services, then legally we can build on existing systems and traditions to evolve a new kind of regulatory service commission to carry out that end. To ensure that the critical legal rights of parents and children are protected, civil family courts—as in foster and adoption cases—would be available for contest and appeal. However, to ensure that the agencies did not become bureaucratic busybodies, additional thought would have to be given to their policy-making composition, staffing and location.

A major deficiency of many regulatory agencies in this country is that special interests often dominate the administration and proceedings, while affected consumers are only sparsely represented. To ensure that the residents most affected by proposed family and child welfare boards had a major voice in the administration and proceedings, they could be set up with a majority of citizen representatives (including adolescents). In addition, they could be decentralized to function within the geographical boundaries of areas the size of local elementary or junior high school districts. These local boards would be granted the legal rights to hire lay and professional staff, as well as to supervise the administration of hearings and field services.

The setting up of these local boards would require an extensive examination of city, county and state child welfare services to ensure effective cooperation and integration of effort. It is certainly conceivable that many existing family and child welfare services, which are generally administered without citizen advice, could also be incorporated into the activities of the local boards. The problems to be ironed out would of course be substantial, but the effort could force a reconceptualization of local and state responsibilities for providing acceptable, humane and effective family and child welfare services on a broad scale.

CITIZEN INVOLVEMENT

The employment of interested local citizens in the daily operation of family and child welfare services is not a totally new idea. Sweden has used local welfare boards to provide a range of services to families and children, including the handling of delinquency cases. While we do not have to copy their broad jurisdictional scope or underrepresentation of blue-collar citizens, a great deal can be learned from this operation. Other Scandinavian countries also use local citizen boards to deal with a range of delinquency offenses. Informed observers indicate that the nonlegal systems in Scandinavia are less primitive and coercive. However, it is difficult to ascertain whether this outcome is due to cultural differences or to the social invention that excludes juvenile courts.

There exists analogues in this country for the use of local citizens in providing services to children in trouble. In recent years there has been an upsurge in the use of citizen-volunteers who function as house parents for home detention facilities, probation officers and intake workers. Besides this use of citizens, New Jersey, for example, has permitted each juvenile court jurisdiction to appoint citizens to Judicial Conference Committees, for the purpose of informally hearing and handling delinquency cases. Some New Jersey counties process up to 50 percent of their court petitions through this alternative to adjudication. All these programs, however, operate under the direct supervision and jurisdiction of the county juvenile court judges, with the cooperation of the chief probation officers. It should be possible to adapt these local innovations to a system that would be independent of the coercive aspects of even the most benign juvenile court operation.

OPPOSITION TO INNOVATION

Quite often it is the powerful opposition of special interest groups, rather than an inability to formulate new and viable proposals for change, that can block beneficial social change. Many judges, probation workers, correction officers, as well as religious and secular child care agencies, would strenuously oppose new social policies and alternatives for handling delinquents without crimes. Their opposition would certainly be understandable, since the proposed changes could have a profound impact on their work. In the process of limiting jurisdiction and altering traditional practices, they could lose status, influence and control over the use of existing resources. Very few interest groups suffer these kinds of losses gladly. Proponents of change should try to understand their problem and act accordingly. However, the differential benefits that might accrue to children and their families should serve as a reminder that the problems of youth and their official and unofficial adult caretakers are not always identical.

EXPERTS' CLAIMS

One proposal in particular can be expected to call forth the ire of these groups, and that is the use of citizens in the administration and provision of services in local boards. Many professional groups—psychiatrists, social workers, psychologists, group therapists and school guidance counselors—have staked out a claim of expertise for the treatment of any "acting out" behavior. The suggestion that citizens should play a significant role in offering assistance undermines that claim. In reply, the professionals might argue that experts—not laymen—should control, administer and staff any programs involving the remediation of childhood troubles. On what grounds might this kind of claim be reasonably questioned?

First, there is nothing about local citizens' control of child and family welfare activities that precludes the hiring of professionals for key tasks, and entrusting them with the operation of the board's program. Many private and public boards in the fields of correction and child welfare have functioned this way in the past.

Second, any claims about an expertise that can be termed a scientific approach to correction are quite premature. There does not now exist a clear-cut body of knowledge that can be ordered in a text or verbally transmitted that will direct any trained practitioner to diagnose and treat effectively such classic problems as truancy, running away and precocious sex experimentation. Unlike the field of medicine, there are no clear-cut prescriptions for professional behavior that can provide an intellectual rationale for expecting a remission of symptoms. There exist bits and pieces of knowledge and practical wisdom, but there is no correctional technology in any acceptable scientific sense.

Third, a reasonable appraisal of evaluations of current approaches to delinquents indicates that there are, in fact, no programs that can claim superiority. The studies do indicate that we can institutionalize far fewer children in treatment centers or reform schools without increasing the risks for individuals or communities; or, if we continue to use institutional programs, young people can be held for shorter periods of time without increasing the risk. The outcome of these appraisals provides a case for an expansion of humane child care activities—not for or against any specific repertoire of intervention techniques.

Fourth, many existing correctional programs are not now controlled by professionals. Untrained juvenile court judges are administratively responsible for detention programs and probation services in more than a majority of the 50 states. Many correctional programs have been headed by political appointees or nonprofessionals. And state legislatures, often dominated by rural legislators, have exercised a very strong influence in the permissible range of program alternatives.

Fifth, the professionalization of officials dealing with delinquent youth does not always lead to happy results. There are studies that indicate that many trained policemen and judges officially process and detain more young people than untrained officials, indicating that their definition of delinquency has been broadened by psychiatric knowledge. At this point in time, there is a distinct danger that excessive professionalization can lead to overintervention in the lives of children and their families.

Sixth, there is no assurance that professionals are any more responsive to the interests and desires of local residents than are untrained judges and probation officers. Citizens, sharing a similar life style and knowledgeable about the problems of growing up in a given community, may be in a better position to enact a *parens patriae* doctrine than are professionals or judges.

Seventh, in ghetto communities, reliance on professional expertise can mean continued dependence on white authority systems. Identification of family and child welfare boards as "our own" may compensate for any lack of expertise by removing the suspicion that any change of behavior by children and parents is for the benefit of the white establishment. The additional community benefits to be gained from caring for "our own" may also outweigh any loss of professional skills. The benefits accruing from indigenous control over local child welfare services would hold for other minority groups living in a discriminatory environment: Indians, Puerto Ricans, Mexicans, hillbillies and French Canadians.

ALTERNATIVE POLICY PROPOSALS

The proposal to create family and child welfare boards to deal with juvenile status offenses may be appealing to many people. However, gaining political acceptance may be quite difficult, since the juvenile justice system would be giving up coercive power in an area that it has controlled for a long period of time. The proposal may appear reasonable, but it may constitute too radical a break with the past for a majority of state legislators. In addition, the interest groups that might push for it are not readily visible. Perhaps participants in the Women's Lib movement, student activists and black power groups might get interested in the issue of injustice against youth, but this is a hope more than a possibility. In the event of overwhelming opposition, there exist two policy proposals that might be more acceptable and could aid in the decriminalization of juvenile status offenses.

The two alternatives function at different ends of the traditional juvenile justice system. One proposal, suggested by the President's Task Force on Delinquency, would set up a Youth Service Bureau that would offer local field services and be operated by civil authorities as an alternative to formal adjudication; the second proposal, suggested by William Sheridan of the Department of Health, Education and Welfare, would prohibit the mixing of juvenile status offenders and classic delinquents in the same institutions. The Youth Service Bureau would function after judicial disposition. Both proposals, separate or in concert, could aid in the decriminalization of our current practices.

However, both proposals would still leave open the possibility of stigmatization of youth who had committed no crimes. The Youth Service Bureau would provide an array of services at the community level, but the court would still have ultimate jurisdiction over its case load, and any competition over jurisdiction would probably be won by the traditional court system. The prohibition of mixing in institutions would, of course, not change the fact that young people were still being adjudicated in the same court as delinquents, even though they had committed no crimes. In addition, the proposal, as currently conceived, does not affect mixing in detention facilities. These limitations are evident in the statutes of states that have recently changed their definitions of "delinquency" (New York, California, Illinois, Colorado, Kansas, Oklahoma and Vermont).

Both proposals deserve support, but they clearly leave the traditional system intact. It is possible that Youth Service Bureaus could be organized with a significant role for citizen participation, thus paving the way for an eventual take-over of legal jurisdiction from the juvenile court for juvenile status offenses (and dependency and neglect cases, too). It is conceivable, too, that any prohibitions of mixing could lead to the increased placement of children in trouble in foster homes and group homes, instead of reform schools, and to the provision of homemaker services and educational programs for harried parents unable to cope with the problems of children. Both short-range proposals could, in practice, evolve a different mode of handling delinquents without crimes.

The adaptation of these two reasonable proposals into an evolutionary strategy is conceivable. But it is also likely they will just be added to the system, without altering its jurisdiction and its stigmatic practices. In the event this occurs, new reformers might entertain the radical strategy that some European countries achieved many years ago—removal of juvenile status offenders from the jurisdiction of the judicial-correctional system and their inclusion into the family and child welfare system.

NEW DEFINITIONS

What is the guarantee that young people will be serviced any more effectively by their removal from the traditional correctional system? The question is valid, but perhaps it underestimates the potency of social definitions. Children, as well as adults, are liable to be treated according to the social category to which they have been assigned. Any shift in the categorization of youth that yields a more positive image can influence such authorities as teachers, employers, military recruiters and housing authority managers. For there is abundant evidence that the stigma of delinquency can have negative consequences for an individual as an adult, as well as during childhood.

It is evident, too, that our old social definitions of what constitutes delinquency have led us to construct a system of juvenile justice that is quite unjust. By failing to make reasonable distinctions and define them precisely, we not only treat juvenile status offenders more harshly but undermine any semblance of ordered justice for *all* illegal behavior committed by juveniles. Maintenance of existing jurisdictional and definitional boundaries helps to perpetuate an unjust system for treating children. That this unjust system may also be a self-defeating one that compounds the original problem should also be taken into account before prematurely concluding that a shift in social labeling procedures is but a minor reform.

We would agree, however, with the conclusion that a mere semantic shift in the social definition of children in trouble is not sufficient. The experience of New York in providing a social label of "person in need of supervision" (PINS)—without providing alternative civil modes for responding to this new distinction—indicates that reform can sometimes take the guise of "word magic." Children are often accused of believing in the intrinsic power of words and oaths; adults can play the game on an even larger scale.

We need alternative social resources for responding to our change in social definitions, if we are at all serious about dealing with the problem. Whether we are willing to pay the financial costs for these alternatives is, of course, problematic. While we have not conducted a financial cost-benefit analysis, it is conceivable that the old system might be cheaper, even though its social costs outweigh any social benefits. Whether we will be willing to tax ourselves to support a more reasonable and moral social policy may turn out to be a critical issue. Perceived in this manner, the problem of children in trouble is as much financial as it is political. This, too, is part of the American approach to juvenile status offenders.

CHILDREN AND THEIR CARETAKERS

Norman K. Denzin

Schools are held together by intersecting moral, political and social orders. What occurs inside their walls must be viewed as a product of what the participants in this arena bring to it, be they children, parents, instructors, administrators, psychologists, social workers, counselors or politicians. A tangled web of interactions—based on competing ideologies, rhetorics, intents and purposes—characterizes everyday life in the school. Cliques, factions, pressure groups and circles of enemies daily compete for power and fate in these social worlds.

Children and their caretakers are not passive organisms. Their conduct reflects more than responses to the pressures of social systems, roles, value structures or political ideologies. Nor is their behavior the sole product of internal needs, drives, impulses or wishes. The human actively constructs lines of conduct in the face of these forces and as such stands over and against the external world. The human is self-conscious. Such variables as role prescription, value configurations or hierarchies of needs have relevance only when they are acted on by the human. Observers of human behavior are obliged to enter the subject's world and grasp the shifting definitions that give rise to orderly social behavior. Failing to do so justifies the fallacy of objectivism: the imputing of motive from observer to subject. Too many architects of schools and education programs have stood outside the interactional worlds of children and adults and attempted to legislate their interpretation of right and proper conduct.

Such objectivistic stances have given schools a basic characteristic that constitutes a major theme of this essay. Schools are presently organized so as to effectively remove fate control from those persons whose fate is at issue, that is, students. This loss of fate control, coupled with a conception of the child which is based on the "underestimation fallacy" gives rise to an ideology that judges the child as incompetent and places in the hands of the adult primary responsibility for child-caretaking.

SCHOOLS AS MORAL AGENCIES

Schools are best seen, not as educational settings, but as places where fate, morality and personal careers are created and shaped. Schools are moral institutions. They have assumed the responsibility of shaping children, of whatever race or income level, into right and proper participants in American society, pursuing with equal vigor the abstract goals of that society.

At one level schools function, as Willard Waller argued in 1937, to Americanize the young. At the everyday level, however, abstract goals disappear, whether they be beliefs in democracy and equal opportunity or myths concerning the value of education for upward mobility. In their place appears a massive normative order that judges the child's development along such dimensions as poise, character, integrity, politeness, deference, demeanor, emotional control, respect for authority and serious commitment to classroom protocol. Good students are those who reaffirm through their daily actions the moral order of home, school and community.

To the extent that schools assume moral responsibility for producing social beings, they can be seen as agencies of fate or career control. In a variety of ways schools remind students who they are and where they stand in the school's hierarchy. The school institutionalizes ritual turning points to fill this function: graduations, promotions, tests, meetings with parents, open-houses, rallies and sessions with counselors. These significant encounters serve to keep students in place. Schools function to sort and filter social selves and to set these selves on the proper moral track, which may include recycling to a lower grade, busing to an integrated school or informing a student that he has no chance to pursue a college preparatory program. In many respects schools give students their major sense of moral worth —they shape vocabularies, images of self, reward certain actions and not others, set the stage for students to be thrown together as friends or enemies.

Any institution that assumes control over the fate of others might be expected to be accountable for its actions toward those who are shaped and manipulated. Within the cultures of fate-controlling institutions, however, there appears a vocabulary, a rhetoric, a set of workable excuses and a division of labor to remove and reassign responsibility. For example, we might expect that the division of labor typically parallels the moral hierarchy of the people within the institution, that is, the people assigned the greatest moral worth are ultimately most blameworthy, or most accountable. Usually, however, moral responsibility is reversed. When a teacher in a Head Start program fails to raise the verbal skills of her class to the appropriate level she and the project director might blame each other. But it is more likely that the children, the families of the children or the culture from which the children come will be held responsible. Such is the typical rhetorical device employed in compensatory education programs where the low performances of black children on white middle-class tests is explained by assigning blame to black family culture and family arrangements. Research on the alleged genetic deficiencies of black and brown children is another example of this strategy. Here the scientist acts as a moral entrepreneur, presenting his findings under the guise of objectivity.

WHAT IS A CHILD?

Any analysis of the education and socialization process must begin with the basic question, "what is a child?" My focus is on the contemporary meanings assigned children, especially as these meanings are revealed in preschool and compensatory education programs.

In addressing this question it must be recognized that social objects (such as children) carry no intrinsic meaning. Rather, meaning is conferred by processes of social interaction—by people.

Such is the case with children. Each generation, each social group, every family and each individual develops different interpretations of what a child is. Children find themselves defined in shifting, often contradictory ways. But as a sense of self is acquired, the child learns to transport from situation to situation a relatively stable set of definitions concerning his personal and social identity. Indeed most of the struggles he will encounter in the educational arena fundamentally derive from conflicting definitions of selfhood and childhood.

CHILD PRODUCTION AS STATUS PASSAGE

The movement of an infant to the status of child is a socially constructed event that for most middle-class Americans is seen as desirable, inevitable, irreversible, permanent, long term in effect and accomplished in the presence of "experts" and significant others such as teachers, parents, peers and siblings.

For the white middle-income American the child is seen as an extension of the adult's self, usually the family's collective self. Parents are continually reminded that the way their child turns out is a direct reflection of their competence as socializing agents. These reminders have been made for some time; consider this exhortation of 1849:

> Yes, mothers, in a certain sense, the destiny of a redeemed world is put into your hands; it is for you to say whether your children shall be respectable and happy here, and prepared for a glorious im-

mortality, or whether they shall dishonor you, and perhaps bring your grey hairs in sorrow to the grave, and sink down themselves at last to eternal despair!

If the child's conduct reflects upon the parent's moral worth, new parents are told by Benjamin Spock that this job of producing a child is hard work, a serious enterprise. He remarks in *Baby and Child Care*:

> There is an enormous amount of hard work in child care—preparing the proper diet, washing diapers and clothes, cleaning up messes that an infant makes with his food . . . stopping fights and drying tears, listening to stories that are hard to understand, joining in games and reading stories that aren't very exciting to an adult, trudging around zoos and museums and carnivals . . . being slowed down in housework . . . . Children keep parents from parties, trips, theaters, meetings, games, friends. . . . Of course, parents don't have children because they want to be martyrs, or at least they shouldn't. They have them because they love children and want some of their very own . . . . Taking care of their children, seeing them grow and develop into fine people, gives most parents—despite the hard work—their greatest satisfaction in life. This is creation. This is our visible immortality. Pride in other worldly accomplishments is usually weak in comparison.

Spock's account of the parent-child relationship reveals several interrelated definitions that together serve to set off the contemporary view of children. The child is a possession of the adult, an extension of self, an incompetent object that must be cared for at great cost and is a necessary obligation one must incur if he or she desires visible immortality.

These several definitions of childhood are obviously at work in current educational programs. More importantly, they are grounded in a theory of development and learning that reinforces the view that children are incompetent selves. Like Spock's theory of growth, which is not unlike the earlier proposals of Gesell, contemporary psychological theories see the child in organic terms. The child grows like a stalk of corn. The strength of the stalk is a function of its environment. If that environment is healthy, if the plant is properly cared for, a suitable product will be produced. This is a "container" theory of development: "What you put in determines what comes out." At the same time, however, conventional wisdom holds that the child is an unreliable product. It cannot be trusted with its own moral development. Nor can parents. This business of producing a child is serious and it must be placed in the hands of experts who are skilled in child production. Mortal mothers and fathers lack these skills. Pressures are quickly set in force to move the child out of the family into a more "professional" setting—the preschool, the Head Start program.

CARETAKING FOR THE MIDDLE CLASSES

Preschools, whether based on "free school" principles, the Montessori theory, or modern findings in child development, display one basic feature. They are moral caretaking agencies that undertake the fine task of shaping social beings.

Recently, after the enormous publicity attendant to the Head Start program for the poor, middle-income Americans have been aroused to the importance of preschool education for their children. "Discovery Centers" are appearing in various sections of the country and several competing national franchises have been established. Given names such as We Sit Better, Mary Moppit, Pied Piper Schools, Les Petites Academies, Kinder Care Nursery and American Child Centers, these schools remind parents (as did the Universal Education Corporation in *The New York Times*) that:

> Evaluating children in the 43 basic skills is part of what the Discovery Center can do for your child. The 43 skills embrace all the hundreds of things your child has to learn before he reaches school age. Fortunately preschoolers have a special genius for learning. But it disappears at the age of seven. During this short-lived period of genius, the Discovery Center helps your child develop his skills to the Advanced Level.

Caretaking for the middle classes is a moral test. The parent's self is judged by the quality of the product. If the product is faulty, the producer is judged inadequate, also faulty. This feature of the socialization process best explains why middle-class parents are so concerned about the moral, spiritual, psychological and social development of their children. It also explains (if only partially) why schools have assumed so much fate control over children; educators are the socially defined experts on children.

The children of lower income families are often assumed to be deprived, depressed and emotionally handicapped. To offset these effects, current theory holds that the child must be "educated and treated" before entrance into kindergarten. If middle-income groups have the luxury of withholding preschool from their children, low-income, third-world parents are quickly learning they have no such right. Whether they like it or not, their children are going to be educated. When formal education begins, the culturally deprived child will be ready to compete with his white peers.

WHAT IS CULTURAL DEPRIVATION?

The term "culturally deprived" is still the catchall phrase which at once explains and describes the inability (failure, refusal) of the child in question to display appropriate conduct on I.Q. tests, street corners, playgrounds and classrooms. There are a number of problems with this formulation. The first is conceptual and involves the meanings one gives to the terms *culture* and *deprived*. Contemporary politicians and educators have ignored the controversy surrounding what the word *culture* means and have apparently assumed that everyone knows what a culture is. Be that as it may, the critical empirical indicator seems to be contained in the term *deprived*. People who are deprived, that is, people who fail to act like white, middle-income groups, belong to a culture characterized by such features as divorce, deviance, premarital pregnancies, extended families, drug addiction and alcoholism. Such persons are easily identified: they tend to live in ghettos or public housing units, and they tend to occupy the lower rungs of the occupation ladder. They are there because they are deprived. Their culture keeps them deprived. It is difficult to tell whether these theorists feel that deprivation precedes or follows being in a deprived culture. The causal links are neither logically or empirically analyzed.

The second problem with this formulation is moral and ideological. The children and adults who are labeled culturally deprived are those people in American society who embarrass and cause trouble for middle-income moralists, scientists, teachers, politicians and social workers. They fail to display proper social behavior. The fact that people in low-income groups are under continual surveillance by police and social workers seems to go unnoticed. The result is that members of the middle class keep their indelicacies behind closed doors, inside the private worlds of home, office, club and neighbor-hood. Low-income people lack such privileges. Their misconduct is everybody's business.

The notion of cultural deprivation is class based. Its recurrent invocation, and its contemporary institutionalization in compensatory education programs reveals an inability or refusal to look seriously at the problems of the middle and upper classes, and it directs attention away from schools, which are at the heart of the problem.

Herbert Gans has noted another flaw in these programs. This is the failure of social scientists to take seriously the fact that many lower-income people simply do not share the same aspirations as the middle class. Despite this fact antipoverty programs and experiments in compensatory education proceed as if such were the case.

Schools are morally bounded units of social organization. Within and from them students, parents, teachers and administrators derive their fundamental sense of self. Any career through a school is neces-sarily moral; one's self-image is continually being evaluated, shaped and molded. These careers are interactionally interdependent. What a teacher does affects what a child does and vice versa. To the extent that schools have become the dominant socializing institution in West-ern society it can be argued that experiences in them furnish everyday interactants with their basic vocabularies for evaluating self and oth-ers. Persons can mask, hide or fabricate their educational biography, but at some point they will be obliged to paint a picture of how well educated they are. They will also be obliged to explain why they are not better educated (or why they are too well educated), and why their present circumstances do not better reflect their capabilities (e.g., unemployed space engineers). One's educational experiences furnish the rhetorical devices necessary to get off the hook and supply the basic clues that will shore up a sad or happy tale.

THE SCHOOL'S FUNCTIONS

I have already noted two broad functions served by the schools: they Americanize students, and they sort, filter and accredit social selves. To these basic functions must be added the following. Osten-sibly, instruction or teaching should take precedence over political so-cialization. And indeed teaching becomes the dominant activity through which the school is presented to the child. But if schools function to instruct, they also function to entertain and divert students into "worthwhile" ends. Trips to zoos, beaches, operas, neighboring towns, ice cream parlors and athletic fields reveal an attempt on the part of the school to teach the child what range of entertaining activities he or she can engage in. Moreover, these trips place the school directly in the public's eye and at least on these excursions teachers are truly held accountable for their class's conduct.

Caretaking and babysitting constitute another basic function of schools. This babysitting function is quite evident in church oriented summer programs where preschools and day-care centers are explicitly oriented so as to sell themselves as competent babysitters. Such schools compete for scarce resources (parents who can afford their services), and the federal government has elaborated this service through grants-in-aid to low-income children.

Formal instruction in the classroom is filtered through a series of interconnected acts that involve teacher and student presenting different social selves to one another. Instruction cannot be separated from social interaction, and teachers spend a large amount of time teaching students how to be proper social participants. Coaching in the rules and rituals of polite etiquette thus constitutes another basic function of the school. Students must be taught how to take turns, how to drink out of cups and clean up messes, how to say please and thank you, how to take leave of a teacher's presence, how to handle mood, how to dress for appropriate occasions, how to be rude, polite, attentive, evasive, docile, aggressive, deceitful; in short, they must learn to act like adults. Teachers share this responsibility with parents, often having to take over where parents fail or abdicate, though, again, parents are held accountable for not producing polite children. Because a child's progress through the school's social structure is contingent on how his or her self is formally defined, parents stand to lose much if their children do not conform to the school's version of good conduct. When teachers and parents both fail, an explanation will be sought to relieve each party of responsibility. The child may be diagnosed as hyperactive, or his culture may have been so repressive in its effects that nothing better can be accomplished. Career tracks for these students often lead to the trade school or the reformatory.

Another function of the schools is socialization into age-sex roles. Girls must be taught how to be girls and boys must learn what a boy is. In preschool and day-care centers this is often difficult to accomplish because bathrooms are not sex segregated. But while they are open territories, many preschools make an effort to hire at least one male instructor who can serve as male caretaker and entertainer of boys. He handles their toilet problems among other things. Preschool instructors can often be observed to reinterpret stories to fit their conception of the male or female role, usually attempting to place the female on an equal footing with the male. In these ways the sexual component of self-identity is transmitted and presented to the young child. Problem children become those who switch sex roles or accentuate to an unacceptable degree maleness or femaleness.

Age-grading is accomplished through the organization of classes on a biological age basis. Three-year-olds quickly learn that they cannot do the same things as four-year-olds do, and so on. High schools are deliberately organized so as to convey to freshmen and sophomores how important it is to be a junior or senior. Homecoming queens, student body presidents and athletic leaders come from the two top classes. The message is direct: work hard, be a good student and you too can be a leader and enjoy the fruits of age.

It has been suggested by many that most schools centrally function to socialize children into racial roles, stressing skin color as the dominant variable in social relationships. Depictions of American history and favored symbolic leaders stress the three variables of age, sex and race. The favored role model becomes the 20- to 25-year-old, white, university-educated male who has had an outstanding career in athletics. Implicitly and explicitly students are taught that Western culture is a male oriented, white-based enterprise.

Shifting from the school as a collectivity to the classroom, we find that teachers attempt to construct their own versions of appropriate conduct. Students are likely to find great discrepancies between a school's formal codes of conduct and the specific rules they encounter in each of their courses and classes. They will find some teachers who are openly critical of the school's formal policies, while at the same time they are forced to interact with teachers who take harsh lines toward misconduct. They will encounter some teachers who enforce dress standards and some who do not. Some teachers use first names, othes do not, and so on. The variations are endless.

The importance of these variations for the student's career and self-conception should be clear. It is difficult managing self in a social world that continually changes its demands, rewards and rules of conduct. But students are obliged to do just that. Consequently the self-conception of the student emerges as a complex and variegated object. He or she is tied into competing and complementary worlds of influence and experience. Depending on where students stand with respect to the school's dominant moral order, they will find their self-conception complemented or derogated and sometimes both. But for the most part schools are organized so as to complement the self-conception of the child most like the teacher and to derogate those most unlike him or her. And, needless to say, the moral career of the non-white, low-income student is quite different from the career of his white peer.

I have spelled out the dimensions around which a student comes to evaluate himself in school. Classrooms, however, are the most vivid stage on which students confront the school, and it is here that the teacher at some level must emerge as a negative or positive force on his career. While the underlife of schools reflects attempts to "beat" or "make-out" in the school, in large degree the student learns to submit to the system. The ultimate fact of life is that unless he gets through school with some diploma he is doomed to failure. Not only is he doomed to failure but he is socially defined as a failure. His career opportunities and self-conceptions are immediately tied to his success in school.

Schools, then, inevitably turn some amount of their attention to the problem of socializing students for failure. Indeed, the school's success as a socializing agent in part depends on its ability to teach students to accept failure. A complex rhetoric and set of beliefs must be instilled in the students. Children must come to see themselves as the school defines them. They are taught that certain classes of selves do better than other classes, but the classes referred to are not sociological but moral. A variation of the Protestant ethic is communicated and the fiction of equality in education and politics is stressed. Students must grasp the fact that all that separates them from a classmate who goes to Harvard (when they are admitted to a junior college) are grades and hard work, not class, race, money or prestige. Schools, then, function as complex, cooling out agencies.

Two problems are created. School officials must communicate

their judgments, usually cast as diagnoses, prescriptions, treatments and prognoses, to students and parents. And second, they must establish social arrangements that maximize the likelihood that their judgments will be accepted, that is, submission to fate control is maximized, and scenes between parents and students are minimized.

FATE CONTROL

The most obvious cooling out agents in schools are teachers and counselors. It is they who administer and evaluate tests. It is they who see the student most frequently. In concert these two classes of functionaries fulfill the schools' functions of sorting out and cooling out children. Their basic assignment is to take imperfect selves and fit those selves to the best possible moral career. They are, then, moral entrepreneurs. They design career programs and define the basic contours around which a student's self will be shaped.

A basic strategy of the moral entrepreneur in schools is co-optation. He attempts to win a child's peers and parents over to his side. If this can be accomplished, the job is relatively easy. For now everyone significant in the child's world agrees that he is a failure or a partial success. They agree that a trade school or a junior college is the best career track to be followed.

Another strategy is to select exemplary students who epitomize the various tracks open to a student. Former graduates may be brought back and asked to reflect on their careers. In selecting types of students to follow these various paths, schools conduct talent searches and develop operating perspectives that classify good and bad prospects. Like the academic theorist of social stratification, these officials work with an implicit image of qualified beings. They know that students from middle- and upper-income groups perform better than those from lesser backgrounds. They know that students who have college educated parents do better than those whose parents dropped out of high school. They learn to mistrust nonwhites. In these respects schools differ only slightly from medical practitioners, especially the psychiatrist who has learned that his trade works best on persons like him in background. Teachers too perpetuate the system of stratification found in the outside world.

STUDENT TYPES

Schools can cool out the failures in their midst. They have more difficulty with another type of student, the troublemakers or militants. Troublemakers, as would be predicted, typically come from low-income white and nonwhite ethnic groups. Forced to process these children, school systems developed their own system of stratification, making low-status schools teach troublemakers. This has become the fate of the trade school or the continuation high school. Here those who have high truancy or arrest records, are pregnant, hyperactive or on probation are thrown together. And here they are presented with white middle-class curriculums.

Militants and troublemakers refuse to accept the school's operating perspective. To the extent that they can band together and form a common world view, they challenge the school's legitimacy as a socializing agent. They make trouble. They represent, from the middle-class point of view, failures of the socializing system.

In response to this, schools tend to adopt a strategy of denial. Denial can take several forms, each revealing a separate attempt to avoid accountability. Denial of responsibility takes the form of a claim that "we recognize your problem, but the solution is outside our province." The need for alternative educational arrangements is recognized, but denied because of reasons beyond control. Private and public guilt is neutralized by denying responsibility and placing blame on some external force or variable such as the state of the economy.

When some resource is denied to a social group, explanations will be developed to justify that denial. My earlier discussion has suggested that one explanation places blame on the shoulders of the denied victim. Thus the theory of cultural deprivation removes blame, by blaming the victim. Scientific theory thus operates as one paradigm of responsibility.

Another form of the strategy is to deny the challengers' essential moral worth. Here the victim is shown to be socially unworthy and thereby not deserving of special attention. This has been the classic argument for segregation in the South, but it works only so long as the victim can be kept in place, which has lately in that part of the world involved insuring that the challenger or victim is not presented with alternative self-models. Shipping black instructors out of the South into northern urban ghettos represents an attempt to remove alternative self-models for the southern black child.

THE VICTIM'S RESPONSE

Insofar as they can organize themselves socially, victims and challengers may assume one of three interrelated stances. They may condemn the condemner, make appeals to higher authorities or deny the perspective that has brought injury. In so doing they will seek and develop alternative scientific doctrines that support their stance.

Condemning the condemner reverses the condemner's denial of moral worth. Here the school or political and economic system is judged hypocritical, corrupt, stupid, brutal and racist. These evaluations attempt to reveal the underlying moral vulnerability of the institution in question. The victim and his cohort reverse the victimizer's vocabulary and hold him accountable for the failures they were originally charged with (for example, poor grades or attendance records).

These condemnations reveal a basic commitment to the present system. They are claims for a just place. They are a petition to higher authority. Democratic ideology is proclaimed as a worthy pursuit. The school is charged with failure to offer proper and acceptable means to reach those goals. Here the victims' perspective corresponds with dominant cultural ideologies.

Denial of perspective is another stance. Best seen in the Nation of Islam schools, the victim now states that he wants nothing the larger system can offer. He leaves the system and constructs his own educational arrangements. He develops his own standards of evaluation. He paints his own version of right and proper conduct. (Private educational academies in the South, partly a function of the Nixon administration, serve a similar function for whites.)

Denials of perspective thus lead to the substitution of a new point of view. If successfully executed, as in the case of the Nation of Islam, the victims build their own walls of protection and shut off the outside world. In such a setting, one's self-conception is neither daily denied nor derided. It is affirmed and defined in positive terms.

Lower self-conceptions would be predicted in those settings where the black or brown child is taught to normalize his deficiencies and to compensate for them. This is the setting offered by Head Start and Follow-Through. The victim accepts the victimizers' judgments and attempts to compensate for socially defined flaws.

Americans of all income levels and from all racial groups, including white, are troubled over the current educational system. They are demanding a greater say in the social organization of schools; they are challenging the tenure system now given teachers; they feel that schools should accept greater responsibilities for the failures of the system. (A Gallup Poll in late 1970 showed that 67 percent of those surveyed favor holding teachers and administrators more accountable for the progress of students.) Accordingly it is necessary to consider a series of proposals that would bring education more in line with cultural and social expectations.

From this perspective education must be grounded in principles that recognize the role of the self in everyday conduct. The child possesses multiple selves, each grounded in special situations and special circles of significant others. Possessing a self, the child is an active organism, not a passive object into which learning can be poured.

Conventional theories of learning define the child as a passive organism. An alternative view of the social act of learning must be developed. George Herbert Mead's analysis provides a good beginning. Creativity or learning occurred, Mead argued, when the individual was forced to act in a situation where conventional lines of conduct were no longer relevant. Following Dewey's discussion of the blocked act, Mead contended that schools and curricula must be organized in ways that challenge the child's view of the world. Standard curricula are based on an opposite view of the human. Redundancy, constant rewards and punishments, piecemeal presentation of materials, and defining the child as incompetent or unable to provoke his own acts best characterizes these programs. Course work is planned carefully in advance and study programs are assiduously followed. The teacher, not the child, is defined as the ultimate educational resource. Parents and local community groups, because they tend to challenge the school's operating perspective, are treated only ritualistically at P.T.A. meetings, open houses, school plays, athletic contests. Their point of view, like the child's, is seldom taken seriously. They are too incompetent. Taking them seriously would force a shift in existing power arrangements in the school.

Mead's perspective proposes just the opposite view of parents, children and education. Education, he argued, is an unfolding, social process wherein the child comes to see himself in increasingly more complex ways. Education leads to self-understanding and to the acquisition of the basic skills. This principle suggests that schools must be socially relevant. They must incorporate the social world of child and community into curriculum arrangements. Cultural diversity must be stressed. Alternative symbolic leaders must be presented, and these must come from realistic worlds of experience. (Setting an astronaut as a preferred "self-model" for seven-year-old males, as a present textbook does, can hardly be defined as realistic). Problematic situations from the child's everyday world must be brought into the classroom. Mead, for example, proposed as early as 1908 that schools teach sex education to children.

Children and parents, then, must be seen as resources around which education is developed and presented. They must be taken seriously. This presupposes a close working relationship between home and school. Parents must take responsibility for their children's education. They can no longer afford to shift accountability to the schools. This simple principle suggests that ethnic studies programs should have been central features of schools at least 50 years ago. Schools exist to serve their surrounding communities, not bend those communities to their perspective.

REDEFINING SCHOOLS

If this reciprocal service function is stressed, an important implication follows. Schools should educate children in ways that permit them to be contributing members in their chosen worlds. Such basics as reading, writing and counting will never be avoided. But their instruction can be made relevant within the worlds the child most directly experiences. This suggests, initially at least, that black and brown children be taught to respect their separate cultural heritages. Second, it suggests that they will probably learn best with materials drawn from those cultures. Third, it suggests that they must be presented with self-models who know, respect and come from those cultures—black teachers must not be removed from southern schools.

To the extent that schools and teachers serve as referent points for the child's self-conception it can be argued that it is not the minority student who must change. But instead it is the white middle-class child who must be exposed to alternative cultural perspectives. Minority teachers must be made integral components of all phases of the educational act.

Mead's perspective suggests, as I have attempted to elaborate, that the classroom is an interactive world. Research by Roger G. Barker and Paul V. Gump on big schools and little schools supports this position and their findings suggest an additional set of proposals. Briefly, they learned that as class and school size increases student satisfaction decreases. Teaching becomes more mechanized, students become more irrelevant and activities not related to learning attain greater importance, social clubs, for example. In short, in big schools students are redundant.

Classroom size and school size must be evaluated from this perspective. If schools exist to serve children and their parents, then large schools are dysfunctional. They are knowledge factories, not places of learning or self-development. Culturally heterogeneous, small-sized classes must be experimented with. Students must have opportunities to know their teachers in personal, not institutional terms. Students must be taught to take one another seriously, not competitively. Small, ecologically intimate surroundings have a greater likelihood of promoting these arrangements than do large-scale, bureaucratically organized classes.

At present, standardized, state and nationally certified tests are given students to assess their psychological, emotional, intellectual and social development. Two problems restrict the effectiveness of these methods, however. With few exceptions they have been standardized on white middle-class populations. Second, they are the only measurement techniques routinely employed.

A number of proposals follow from these problems. First, open-ended tests which permit the child to express his or her perspective must be developed. These tests, such as the "Who Am I?" question, would be given to students to determine the major contours of their self-conceptions. With this information in hand teachers would be in a better position to tailor teaching programs to a child's specific needs, definitions, intentions and goals.

Second, tests such as "Who is Important to You?" could be given students on a regular basis to determine who their significant others are. It is near axiomatic that derogation of the people most important to one leads to alienation from the setting and spokesman doing the derogation. Teachers must learn to respect and present in respectful terms those persons most important to the child.

A third methodological proposal directs observers to link a student's utterances, wishes and self-images to his or her day-to-day conduct. Written test scores often fail to reflect what persons really take into account and value. In many social settings verbal ability, athletic skill, hustling aptitudes, money and even physical attractiveness serve as significant status locators. I.Q. tests often do not. Furthermore, a person's score on a test may not accurately reflect his ability to handle problematic situations, which is surely a goal of education. Observations of conduct (behavior) in concrete settings can provide the needed leads in this direction.

METHODOLOGICAL IMPLICATIONS

A critic of these proposals might remark that such measures are not standardized, that their validity is questionable, that they cannot be administered nationally, and that they have questionable degrees of reliability. In response I would cite the ability of Roger Barker and colleagues to execute such observations over time with high reliability (.80–.98 for many measures). But more to the point I would argue that conventional tests are simply not working and it is time to experiment with alternative techniques, perspectives and theories.

This defense suggests that schools of education must begin to consider teaching their students the methodologies of participant observation, unobtrusive analysis and life history construction. These softer methods have been the traditional province of sociologists and anthropologists. Members of these disciplines must consider offering cross-disciplinary courses in methodology, especially aimed for everyday practitioners in school settings. Graduate requirements for teaching credentials must also be reexamined and greater efforts must be made to recruit and train minority students in these different approaches.

These proposals reflect a basic commitment. Schools should be organized so as to maximize a child's self-development and they should permit maximum child-parent participation. It is evident that my discussion has not been limited to an analysis of compensatory education programs. This has been deliberate. It is my conviction that education, wherever it occurs, involves interactions between social selves. Taking the self as a point of departure I have attempted to show that what happens to a preschool child is not unlike the moral experiences of a black or brown 17-year-old senior. But most importantly, both should find themselves in schools that take them seriously and treat them with respect. Schools exist to serve children and the public. This charge must also be taken seriously.

HOW SCHOOL STUNTS YOUR CHILD

George B. Leonard

Teachers are overworked and underpaid. True. It is an exacting and exhausting business, this damming up the flood of human potentialities. What energy it takes to turn a torrent into a trickle, to train that trickle along narrow, well-marked channels! Teachers are often tired. In the teachers' lounge, they sigh their relief into stained cups of instant coffee and offer gratitude to whoever makes them laugh at the day's disasters. This laughter permits a momentary sanity-saving acknowledgment, shared by all, that what passes for humdrum or routine or boring is, in truth, tragic. (An hour, of which some 50 minutes are given up to "classroom control." One child's question unanswered,

"How School Stunts Your Child." From George B. Leonard, *Education and Ecstacy* (New York: Delacorte Press, 1968). Copyright © 1968 by George Leonard. Reprinted by permission of Delacorte Press and The Sterling Lord Agency, Inc.

a hundred unasked. A smart student ridiculed: "He'll learn better."
He learns.) Sweet laughter, shooting up like artesian water, breaks
through encrusted perceptions and leaves a tear in the teacher's eye.
A little triumph.

How do teachers bear their tragic task? They learn to look away.
They hasten to a way of talking that lets them forget their problems.
What cannot be solved is named. Once named, it does not seem to
need a solution so urgently—perhaps never. James "acts out." (He is
mad as hell at his teacher.) Melissa is an "underachiever." (So be it.)
Some teachers take to acting. They generally enter this calling in the
later grades, where the lecture system (best way to get information
from teacher's notebook to student's notebook without touching the
student's mind) flowers fully. Retiring behind a psychic proscenium
arch, the actor-teacher is forever safe. His performance flourishes. He
plays for laughs and outraged looks. Phantom applause accompanies
his trip home to his wife, and he cannot wait to go onstage again.
Assured of a full house and a long run, he knows the critics will be
kind. Those who give him a bad review will get a failing grade.

Principals have another out: their buildings. Concrete, glass,
steel and wood stand still; their problems do not anguish the soul. I
have visited a hundred schools, and it is always the same. The visitor
is directed to the office. There is an exchange of pleasantries, after
which the principal escorts the visitor on a little tour around the plant.
No matter that the visitor may have come only to work with Mrs.
Morrison, the second-grade teacher down the hall. First, the tour.

The principal walks briskly. "This is the multipurpose room.
Notice the flexible dividers." In and out and down a corridor bright
with what he calls "decorator colors." Classroom doors are open, and
the electricity of pent-up life crisscrosses the hall. I am drawn to an
open door. The principal hesitates, then presses on. I follow.

A boy sits on the floor of the hall next to a classroom door, his
back against the wall, his head between his knees. He is a cliché—
sweaty, tousled black hair, loose shirttail, a tennis shoe untied. As we
pass, one big, luminous eye appears between his knuckles and aims an
accusation at me. Why has he been expelled from the company of
his peers? I am drawn to the left. "On the right here is our new teachers' lounge." I go right. "I want you to feel free to use this room any-
time you want. There's always coffee here, or you can just chew the
rag with members of our staff."

We go on, into a classroom at last. It is a fifth grade, presided over by a stout maiden with glasses and reddish hair. Upon our appearance, the electricity within the room changes in a flash; the voltage of tension drops, the amperage of interest rises. Every face turns to us. "Excuse us, Miss Brown. I want our visitor to see one of our new classrooms." At the second seat of the second row, a boy's eyes drop from us to a notebook propped up on his desk. As the principal talks, I drift around to see what the boy is reading. Ah, a copy of *Popular Mechanics* hidden behind the notebook. He glances resentfully at me, then goes on reading, his eyes stubborn and dreamy. An aura of rare intelligence encircles him. I look away. He will need to keep all his stubbornness and all his dreams.

"If you'll notice the placement of the skylight, here, on the side of the room away from the windows, you'll see that the illumination is perfectly balanced at every desk." The principal is happy, and I rejoice with him about the delicious, perfectly balanced flow of outdoor light into a room filled with beautiful children. But something disturbs me, a vinegary tingle at the back of my neck. *There is a witch in this room.* I see her near the back of the fourth row—milk-white skin, black hair falling onto a faded blue blouse, a band of freckles across the bridge of a small, sharp nose. Dark eyes with dilated pupils are fixed on me now, bold and direct, telling me that she knows, without words, everything that needs to be known about me. I return her stare, feeling that this girl, with an education she is not likely to get, might foretell the future, read signs, converse with spirits. In Salem, she eventually would suffer the ordeal of fire and water. In our society, she will be adjusted.

"When it gets dark outside," the principal is saying, "an electric-eye device—here—automatically compensates by turning up the lights." The girl's eyes never leave mine. She is a sorceress, too, for already she has created a whole new world inhabited only by the two of us. It is not a sexual world. What she has in mind—she could never put it into words—bypasses the erotic entirely. But later, when those talents of hers that do not fit the scientific-rationalist frame are finally extinguished, she may turn to sex. And she may become promiscuous, always seeking the shadow of an ecstasy and knowledge that by then she will remember only as a distant vibration, an inexplicable urge toward communion.

"You see, a classrom such as this can never become dark. The illumination will always be even." The principal, I realize, is telling Miss Brown that we are leaving. The girl has no intention of releasing my eyes. The principal is moving toward the door. For a moment, I grow dizzy, then break the connection and follow my host out of the door, quickly reassuming the disguise we all must wear to travel safely in the world that I and the principal and most of us customarily pretend is real.

I compliment the principal, but I know the illumination in that room will never be even. A classroom, any classroom, is an awesome place of shadows and shifting colors, a place of unacknowledged desires and unnamed powers, a magic place. Its inhabitants are tamed. After years of unnecessary repetition, they will be able to perform their tricks—reading, writing, arithmetic and their more complex derivatives. But they are tamed only in the manner of a cageful of jungle cats. Let the right sets of circumstances arise, the classroom will explode.

What a job this is we give our teachers! Do not blame them if they fail to educate, to change their students. For the task of *preventing* the new generation from changing in any deep or signficant way is precisely what most societies require of their educators. They are our valiant slaves, condemned to perpetuate the very system that victimizes them. They are sometimes bewildered, sometimes angry, often tired, because—at a time of harrowing cultural upheaval, with practically an entire continental civilization's children in school—the mutual deception between them and their masters is wearing thin. If education is a process that causes real change, not just in one's ability to manipulate symbols but in every aspect of one's being, then what today's educators are called upon to do may be many things, but it is not education.

And yet, there are moments of learning, even in school. "Have you ever noticed," a teacher said, out of the blue, "how sometimes there are teachable days?" The teachers' lounge fell suddenly silent. "I know sometimes *they* are teachable," a second teacher mused. "Some days, it's different," the first teacher continued. "The whole thing's different. I don't know why."

How many of those times do you remember? *Something happens.* A delicate warmth slides into parts of your being you didn't even realize were cold. The marrow of your bones begins to thaw.

You feel a little lurch, as your own consciousness, the teacher's voice, the entire web of sound and silence that holds the class together, the room itself, the very flow of time all shift to a different level. And suddenly, it is Christmas Morning, with students and teacher exchanging delightful gifts while bells silently chime; the old furniture around the room reflects a holiday gleam; your classmates' eyes sparkle and snap like confetti, and you realize with the certainty of music how rare and valuable each inhabitant of that room has become, has always been. Or you find yourself trembling slightly with the terror and joy of knowledge, the immensity of existence and pattern and change. And when it ends and you must go, you reel from the room with flushed face, knowing you will never again be quite the same. You have learned.

How many teachable days? One out of a hundred? Then you are of the favored.

But there are teachers, a few of them, who can make something happen almost every day. I have seen more than my share of those masters who, in terms of our small expectations, seem to be miraculously gifted. No principal or superintendent misses a chance to show me such a teacher if one is anywhere around. I have sat in a child's miniature chair in the back of a third-grade room, my heart racing, while the class learned simple arithmetic. And I have been changed.

How many such teachers in your lifetime? How many who changed your life? Two? Three? Count yourself lucky.

So here we are. And there our children sit, counting out a few seconds of learning for every hour of waiting for a bell to ring, waiting for a kind of teacher they may have never known, waiting for *something to happen.* If only their waiting could be merely neutral, we wish. If only they could sit there, learning *nothing,* without ill effects! "Look upon every delay as an advantage," Rousseau wrote, "it is gaining a great deal to advance without losing anything." He sought some way "to do nothing yourself, . . . to prevent anything being done by others, . . . to bring up your pupil healthy and robust to the age of twelve years without his being able to distinguish his right hand from his left."

But no one can be rescued from learning; learning is what human life is. Brain researcher John Lilly and others have tried to cut off the connections between the inner self and the world of the senses from which the stuff of learning comes. In these sensory-deprivation experiments, the subject is suspended, nude, in a tank of tepid water. His eyes are blindfolded, his ears are plugged; he breathes through a face mask. He becomes, as far as possible, a disembodied brain. But the brain is not content to rest. It reshuffles past learning, builds rich new inner worlds in which the self seems to move and learn. "When I went in the tank," Dr. Lilly told me, "I could will myself into the center of a giant computer. I could see the connections reaching out from me in every direction in vivid colors. Or, if I wished, I could ski across the top of the Andes, skimming from one peak to another."

There are no neutral moments. Even in those classrooms where the education some of us might hope for is impossible, a kind of shadowy, negative learning is going on. Some pupils learn how to daydream; others, how to take tests. Some learn the petty deceptions involved in cheating; others, the larger deceptions of playing the school game absolutely straight (the well-kept note-book, the right answer, the senior who majors in good grades). Most learn that the symbolic tricks their keepers attempt to teach them have little to do with their own deeper feelings or anything in the here and now. The activity that masquerades under the ancient and noble name of "education" actually seems to serve as a sort of ransom to the future, a down payment toward "getting ahead"—or at least toward not falling behind. Lifetime-earnings figures are pressed upon potential high school dropouts. These figures seem to show that giving an acceptable interpretation of *Ode on a Grecian Urn* means you will live in a better suburb and drive a bigger car. A vision of Florida retirement superimposes itself on every diagram in plane geometry. Some students refuse to pay the ransom, and you should not be surprised that these students may be what society calls the "brighter" ones. But dropouts and graduates alike have had plenty of practice in fragmenting their lives—segregating senses from emotions from intellect, building boxes for art and abstractions, divorcing the self from the reality and the joy of the present moment. No need to look for obscure psychological explanations for modern man's fragmentation; that is what his schools teach.

Over the years, reformers have tried to stop the fragmentation. The greatest among them was John Dewey. Dewey recognized that education is a process of living and not a preparation for living. He believed that education is the fundamental method of social progress and reform.

But Dewey did not provide educators with the hard-honed tools of true reform. He was fascinated with the notion of "interests," which he felt would automatically manifest themselves in children when they were *ready* to learn something. This notion, somewhat misinterpreted, led a generation of teachers to wait for children to show signs of "interest" before they moved ahead and thereby woefully to underrate their capacity for learning. Teachers found further justification for just waiting in the work of developmental psychologists who followed Dewey. These good-hearted doubters are still around, with stacks of studies to show us precisely what children *cannot* do until this age or that age. Their studies become worthless when children are placed in learning environments designed to let them crash through all the ceilings erected by the past. Progressive education was a useful, humane and sometimes joyful reform, but it was not the true revolution in education that the times then needed and now demand. The worst of that movement may be summed up in one sentence: It is as cruel to bore a child as to beat him.

For the most part, the schools have not really changed. They have neither taken up the retreat of the past's prime educators (family, farm, village, church, guild) nor significantly altered the substance and style of their teaching. The most common mode of instruction today, as in the Renaissance, has a teacher sitting or standing before a number of students in a single room, presenting them with facts and techniques of a verbal-rational nature. Our expectation of what the human animal can learn, can do, can be remains remarkably low and timorous. Our definition of education's root purpose remains short-sightedly utilitarian. Our map of the territory of learning remains antiquated: vocational training, homemaking, driving and other "fringe" subjects—themselves limiting and fragmenting—have invaded the curriculum, but are generally considered outside the central domain of "education." This domain, this venerable bastion, is still a place where people are trained to split their world into separate symbolic systems, the better to cope with and manipulate it. Such "education," suprarationalistic and analytical to the extreme, has made possible colonialism, the production line, space voyaging and the H-bomb. But it has not made people happy or whole, nor does it now offer them ways to change, deep down, in an age that cries out with the urgency of a rocket's flight, "Change or die."

All that goes on in most schools and colleges today is only a thin slice of what education can become. And yet, our present institutions show a maddening inefficiency even in dealing with this thin slice. In recent years, there has been a small net gain in U.S. students' performance in the basic subjects. But this has been accomplished only at the cost of a large increase in gross effort—more and more homework assigned under threat of more and tougher exams, to force students to learn, on their own, what most of today's teachers have long since realized they cannot teach them. A visitor from another planet might conclude that our schools are hell-bent on creating—in a society that offers leisure and demands creativity—a generation of joyless drudges.

There are signs the schools will not succeed in this drab mission. Already, the seeds of a real change are germinating—on college campuses, in teachers' associations, in laboratories of science, in out-of-the-way places . . . . This reform would bypass entirely the patchwork remedial measures (Spanish in second grade, teachers in teams, subject matter updated) that presently pass for reform. It cuts straight to the heart of the educational enterprise, in and out of school, seeking new method, content, idiom, domain, purpose and, indeed, a new definition of education. It is a new journey. To join it, you had best leave your awe of history behind, open your mind to unfamiliar solutions, if they are the ones that work, look upon all systems of abstractions as strictly tentative and throw out of the window every prior guideline about what human beings can accomplish.

The prospects are exhilarating, though it is becoming dangerous to write about them, if only because nowadays it is so hard to stay ahead of reality. Let us assume the future will surprise us; and, so assuming, speculate only about what is already coming to pass. For example, the following prospects are in the realm of possibility:

- Ways can be worked out to help average students learn whatever is needed of today's subject matter in a third or less of the time now required, pleasurably rather than painfully, with almost certain success.

- Ways can be worked out to provide a new apprenticeship for living, appropriate to a technological age of constant change. Many new types of learning having to do with crucial areas of human functioning that are now neglected or completely ignored can be made a part of the educational enterprise. Much of what will be learned tomorrow does not today have even a commonly accepted name.

- Ways can be worked out so that almost every day will be a "teachable day," so that almost every educator can share with his students the inspired moments of learning now enjoyed by only the most rare and remarkable.

- Education in a new and greatly broadened sense can become a lifelong pursuit for everyone. To go on learning, to go on sharing that learning with others may well be considered a purpose worthy of mankind's ever-expanding capacities.

If education in the coming age is to be not just a part of life but the main purpose of life, then education's purpose will, at last, be viewed as central. What, then, is the purpose, the goal of education? A large part of the answer may well be what men of this civilization have longest feared and most desired: *the achievement of moments of ecstasy*. Not fun, not simply pleasure, as in the equation of Bentham and Mill, not the libido pleasure of Freud, but ecstasy, *ananda,* the ultimate delight.

Western civilization, for well-known historical reasons, has traditionally eschewed ecstasy as a threat to goal-oriented control of men, matter and energy—and has suffered massive human unhappiness. Other civilizations, notably that of India, have turned their best energies toward the attainment of ecstasy while neglecting practical goals—and have suffered massive human unhappiness. Now, modern science and technology seem to be preparing a situation in which the successful control of practical matters and the attainment of ecstasy can safely coexist; in which each reinforces the other; and in which, quite possibly, neither can long exist *without* the other. Abundance and population control already are logically and technologically feasible. At the same time, cybernation, pervasive and instantaneous communication and other feedback devices of increasing speed, range and sensitivity extend and enhance man's sensory apparatus, multiplying the possibilities for understanding and ecstasy as well as for misunderstanding and destruction. The times demand that we choose delight.

Do discipline and mastery of technique stand in opposition to freedom, self-expression and the ecstatic moment? Most Western educators have acted as if they did. Strange, when there exist so many models of the marriage between the two. Take the artistic endeavor:

The composer discovers that the soul of creation transcends the body of form only when form is his completely. The violinist arrives at the sublime only through utter mastery of technique. The instruments of living that are now coming into our hands—rich, responsive and diverse—require mastery. The process of mastery itself can be ecstatic, leading to delight that transcends mastery.

The new revolutionaires of education must soothe those who fear techniques no less than those who fear delight. Many a liberal educational reform has foundered on lack of specific tools for accomplishing its purposes—even if a tool may be something as simple as knowing *precisely when* to leave the learner entirely alone. Education must use its most powerful servant, technique, in teaching skills that go far beyond those that submit to academic achievement tests. Even today, as will be seen, specific, systematic ways are being worked out to help people learn to love, to feel deeply, to expand their inner selves, to create, to enter new realms of being.

What is education? The answer may be far simpler than we imagine:

To learn is to change. Education is a process that changes the learner.

The first part of our definition of education calls on the educator to view his work as consequential, not theoretical or formalistic. Looking for *change* in his student (and himself) as a measure, he will discover what is important in his work and what is waste motion. Asking himself, "What has changed in the student, and me, because of this particular experience?" he may have to answer that what has changed is only the student's ability to recite a few more "facts" than he could before the session. He may find that the student has changed in wider and deeper ways. He may have to admit that the student has hardly changed at all or, if so, in a way that no one had intended. In any case, he will not ask himself the *wrong* questions ("Wasn't my presentation brilliant?" "Why are they so dumb?").

Looking for the *direction and further consequences* of the change, he will be forced to ask whether it is for the good of the student, himself and society. In doing this, the educator will discover he has to become sensitive to what is happening to the student at every moment, and thereby will become a feeling participant in the circle of learning. Viewing learning as anything that changes the learner's behavior, the educator will expand his domain a thousandfold, for he will realize there are hardly any aspects of human life that cannot be changed, educated. He will see clearly that, if the educational enterprise limits itself to what is now ordinarily taught, it will be pursuing failure in the coming age.

Learning involves interaction between the learner and his environment, and its effectiveness relates to the frequency, variety and intensity of the interaction.

Guided by this second part of the definition, the educator will pay far closer attention to the learning environment than ever before in education's history. The environment may be a book, a game, a programmed device, a choir, a brain-wave feedback mechanism, a silent room, an interactive group of students, even a teacher—but in every case, the educator will turn his attention from mere *presentation* of the environment (a classroom lecture, for example) to the *response* of the learner. He will study and experiment with the learning process, the series of responses, at every step along the way, better to use the increasing capacities of environment and learner as each changes. Observing the work of what have been called "master teachers" in this light, he will find that their mysterious, unfathomable "artistry" actually comprises a heightened sensitivity to student responses plus the use of personally developed, specific, flexible techniques. The educator will work out ways to help every teacher become an "artist."

Education, at best, is ecstatic.

The first two parts of the definition need the third, which may be seen as a way of praising learning for its own sake. And yet, it goes further, for the educator of the coming age will not be vague or theoretical about this matter. As he loses his fear of delight, he will become explicit and specific in his pursuit of the ecstatic moment. At its best, its most effective, its most unfettered, the moment of learning is a moment of delight. This essential and obvious truth is demonstrated for us every day by the baby and the preschool child, by the class of the artist-teacher, by learners of all ages interacting with new learning programs designed for success. When joy is absent, the effectiveness of the learning process falls until the human being is operating hesitantly, grudgingly, fearfully, at only a tiny fraction of his potential.

The notion that ecstasy is mainly an inward-directed experience testifies to our distrust of our own society, of the outer environment we have created for ourselves. Actually, the varieties of ecstasy are limitless. . . . The new educator will seek out the possibility of delight in every form of learning. He will realize that solving an elegant mathematical problem and making love are different classes in the same order of things, sharing common ecstasy. He will find that even education now considered nothing more than present drudgery for future payoff—learning the multiplication tables, for example—can become joyful when a skillfully designed learning environment (a programmed game, perhaps) makes the learning quick and easy. Indeed, the skillful pursuit of ecstasy will make the pursuit of excellence, not for the few, but for the many, what it never has been—successful. And yet, make no mistake about it, excellence, as we speak of it today, will be only a by-product of a greater unity, a deeper delight.

Whenever we do anything about education—whether formally in separate buildings staffed by people called "teachers" or otherwise—we are forced up against the ultimate human questions: What are we? What are we to do with our lives? What specific actions will make it possible for us to do it? We do not always answer these questions with words. Or, if we use words, they often have little to do with the real answers. But the answers are there, acknowledged or not, in every administrative directive, every textbook, every teachers' meeting, every classroom. If we are to have schools in the future, how are they to answer the question of human purpose?

Schools and colleges, until now, have served a society that needed reliable, predictable human components. Appropriately, they have spent overwhelming amounts of time and energy ironing out those human impulses and capabilities that seemed errant. Since learning involves behavioral change, lifelong learning becomes the most errant of behaviors and is not to be countenanced. Educational institutions, therefore, have been geared to *stop* learning. Perhaps half of all learning ability is squelched in the earliest grades, where children find that there exist predetermined, unyielding "right answers" for everything, that following instructions is what counts and, surprisingly, that the whole business of education is mostly dull and painful.

With the bulk of learning ability wiped out in early childhood, the schools can proceed at their own leisure to slow and then still what is left of each human component's capacity to change. The process moves at different rates for different types of components. The simpler ones (unskilled workers, for example) are finished off after only a few years of schooling. More complex components take longer to shape. Schooling's most elegant maneuver consists of braking learning ability so that, for all practical purposes, it will reach zero speed just at the point of graduation. Exceptions are made. Art can be set aside as a sanctuary for lifelong learning. Another activity, generally termed "the life of the mind," has been found to be generally harmless and inconsequential; so it, too, is sanctioned by society even after graduation. Thus, the illusion of lifelong learning can be maintained while the organism changes hardly at all beyond its ability to verbalize "concepts."

The process of formal education itself is kept in motion by punishment or the threat of it, and by two main positive motivators: narrow competition and eager acquisition. These motivators have become answers in themselves to the ultimate questions of life's purpose. Narrow competition, for example, serves ends that go far beyond motivation. It produces close resemblance among those involved. Competition needs specialists who distinguish themselves from one another primarily by doing the *same* thing slightly better or faster. As much as any other factor, it has created the standardization so essential to the highly structured societies of the Civilized Epoch. Individuals who perform unique acts or live unique lives tend to make narrow competition impossible and thereby to throw the traditional social structure out of kilter.

Acquisition, too, serves not only as a motivator but also as a purpose of life. In our own society, acquisition reaches its fullest expression in the accumulation of wealth. (When you ask, "What's Mr. Jones worth?" there's no doubt about what you mean.) Students are prepared for this by the use of symbols—gold stars, class listings, awards. Piling up honors, tangible or intangible, has the effect of divorcing the student from his own feelings, his own being. A man's worth, it might be noted, is measured by things *outside* himself. These things are best mesasured by symbols (words, figures), which helps account for the dominance of symbols over personal feelings in Western civilization.

A society that encourages competition and acquisition is almost sure to encourage aggression—and violence—as well. This may be seen on a national scale in the drive to acquire territory, wealth or status—especially by means of war or colonization. Preparing young men in the behaviors needed for these activities has become perhaps the most powerful shaper of education—and of life's purpose. Conflict is rooted deeply not only in educational practices but in our language itself. We find ourselves engaged in a "War on Poverty," a "battle against discrimination," a "mobilization for peace."

The male bias of education explains a great deal. In order for young men to bear the conditions of war or colonization, it has been necessary that they reduce their imagination and self-awareness to a minimum. One can best live in an alien land, governing an alien race, or fight to the death against an impersonal foe by conceiving oneself as an instrument of something other than oneself. This trick of detachment has been taught in many ways. Stereotyped behavior can be achieved by close-order drill on the parade ground and instructional drill in the classroom. Slogans have justified the behavior. "To die for Rome is noble" said more for Rome than for the Roman soldier. Team games have helped submerge and repudiate individual feelings.

Concentration on technical proficiency has become one of the very best ways to avoid awareness of self. The swordsman in a duel or the jet pilot in a dogfight generally is more concerned with his cold proficiency than with the survival of his own physical person. Detachment from self reaches an extreme in the test pilot. Facing imminent death, he keeps his interest focused on his flight instruments. Millions have heard the voices of astronauts (test pilots all), calm and mechanical in the face of epic dangers. Courage? Yes, but also detachment, divorce from the self. These things can be and are being taught.

I cannot forget the wartime educational procedures that helped me operate successfully while remaining coolly detached from my own deepest feelings—standing at attention for hours in the July Alabama sun in flagrant disregard of the body's urgent messages; learning that "There are only three answers to a superior officer in this man's Air Corps, 'Yes, sir,' 'No, sir,' and 'No excuse, sir' "; practicing in-flight emergency procedures over and again, until they become not merely automatic but entirely impersonal. No, I cannot fault these measures when used in preparation for war, for the precarious conquest of the physical world or for the subduing of alien peoples. For such purposes, they are quite apt. I can wonder, though, at the extent to which they have shaped the entire educational enterprise, for boys and girls alike. Wartime aviation-cadet training was nothing more than prep school exaggerated, and the prep school has long remained a model for the "quality" public school.

"Right answers," specialization, standardization, narrow competition, eager acquisition, aggression, detachment from the self. Without them, it has seemed, the social machinery would break down. Do not call the schools cruel or unnatural for furthering what society has demanded. The reason we now need radical reform in education is that society's demands are changing radically. If education continues along the old tack, humanity sooner or later will simply destroy itself.

To take one example: The narrow competition, eager acquisition and aggression clustered around the manufacture, marketing and purchasing of automobiles in the U.S. have resulted in ever larger and more powerful internal-combustion engines. Dr. Philip Leighton, Professor of Chemistry, Emeritus, of Stanford University, has calculated that just one American car consumes well over a thousand times as much oxygen as does a person. Worse yet, Dr. Leighton writes, "to carry off the exhaust gases, and dilute them to harmless concentrations, requires from five to ten million times as much air as does the driver. In other words, just one automobile, moving along a Los Angeles County freeway, needs as much air to disperse its waste products as do all the people in the County for breathing." The supply of oxygen in the earth's atmosphere is huge, but not unlimited. If the spread of the internal-combustion engines continues at its present rate all over the world, and if the oxygen-producing greenery keeps getting chopped down (to make space for roads, among other things), a time may come when there is simply not enough natural, uncontaminated air to support life.

And this is only one of many ways man is swiftly arranging his own destruction. Mere existence in the largest cities is becoming almost unendurable, even for the most affluent. Air pollution is reaching out and damaging forest greenery in distant mountain ranges. The most beautiful lakes and streams are being poisoned. Lovely hills are being leveled for monotonous house sites. The whole earth is being polluted: The bodies of seals, penguins, skuas and fish in the Antarctic, remote from the source of the poisoning, have been discovered to contain DDT.

"No man is an island" and "All men are brothers" may have been theoretical statements before; now, in the time of worldwide, interlocking, responsive, all-pervasive, powerful technology, they are cries for self-preservation. The regionwide power failures of recent years have given us reminders of our interdependence. During the first great Eastern blackout, New Yorkers found themselves walking down the streets singing with strangers, touching one another. They were reaching for the future.

To die for Rome—or any other state—is no longer noble. It is too easy to take the whole world down with you. The H-bomb is brotherhood's most decisive seal. Peripheral wars, ever more wasteful and frustrating, may go on for years to come. But WAR is through. What justification, then, is there for continuing those educational procedures that prepare the young for the conditions of gross conflict? Even on the most vigilantly maintained first line of national defense, one may now find young Air Force officers sitting at desks in underground silos studying for advanced degrees as they baby-sit their nuclear-tipped missiles.

But how about test pilots? Won't we need cool, detached, icy-eyed young men to complete the conquest of the universe? Perhaps not. Already, the most advanced aircraft are almost totally automated, just as will be the spaceships of the future. Putting men in those U.S. and Russian moon vehicles may turn out to have been, in the scientific community's own frame of reference, a silly salute to the past. Many believe we would have done well to concentrate on much less expensive robot devices with hypersensitive sensors to do our moon exploring for us.

In any case, the age of man as a component—whether of a pyramid-building gang or a space system—is just about over. The future will require that men behave in none of the ways thus far noted. A world in which everyone will be in touch needs people in touch with themselves. Where the actions of one can drastically affect the lives of others far distant, it will be crucially important that each person master the skill of feeling what others feel. This skill, more than new laws or new politics, will soon become crucial to the survival of the race. Such empathy is possible only in one deeply aware of his own feelings. The future will very likely judge nothing less appropriate than detached, fragmented, unfeeling men. Such men have done their work. They have fought wars, built empires. But on a globe newly linked and painfully sensitive to the most distant disturbances, men who conceive of themselves as impersonal instruments can easily become instruments of destruction.

Anyone who thinks that man is "naturally" aggressive should

visit an infantry training school, where the most ingenious, desperate measures are needed to turn young Americans into aggressive killers. (Typical sign in the Fort Ord, Calif., training area: THE SPIRIT OF THE BAYONET IS TO KILL.) But the measures are never altogether successful. Even when killing is socially sanctioned and highly rewarded, even when it may save the soldiers' own lives, many GI's never fire their rifles. During the Korean War, studies show, only one out of four fired during battle.

No, man is not naturally aggressive. "Instincts" are not *needed* to explain those aggressions that do exist. Even if man had not a trace of instinctive aggression, the conditions of civilized living would require that he learn it. As these conditions change, so will man.

The first thing schools can do to reduce narrow competition, eager acquisition and aggression is to stop teaching them. Grades, tests, prizes, honors have proven woefully inadequate as motivators for learning, even at the height of the Civilized Epoch. When learning becomes truly rewarding for its own sake—and this goal has been given lip service for centuries—then narrow competition will be seen for what it is: irrelevant to the learning process and damaging to the development of free-ranging, lifelong learners.

Eager acquisition and aggression may seem more difficult to reduce. Thus far, the emotions and actions associated with them have been highly reinforcing. With life's rewards lodged outside the self, the acquisition of extraneous tangibles or intangibles has naturally been synonymous with success. And, under some circumstances, the behaviors and feelings associated with aggression can be most desirable. The blood runs fast, the senses sharpen, the veil of the commonplace falls away; a man can transcend himself.

Punishing eager acquisition and aggression has never really worked. It has created more scars than cures. It has left a legacy of resentment against social controllers who would quell in others what they themselves live by. Neither punishment nor diversion answers the problem in education. Acquisition will slow when technology creates a condition of plenty rather than deprivation for all. Aggression will quiet down when aggressiveness stops being rewarded.

Still, a faster, more positive remedy is needed. It already is available in the form of an alternative reinforcer that will stir the blood and senses, that will make aggression merely uninteresting. It is joy, delight, ecstasy, the ancient, potent cure so long feared by

Civilization, now so specifically and obviously prescribed. Joy resides *within* the self and is the most relevant of reinforcers.

The emerging mode of life promises to be so challenging, so vivid, so intense as to render the old life extremely dull. The end of the "job" means the end of the eight-hour day and the beginning of the 24-hour day. Lifelong learning, lifelong creative change, is an exhilarating and dangerous endeavor that will require far more human intensity and courage than the old modes.

Freed from the hunter's struggle for survival, freed from the Civilized man's incumbency as specialized component, the human race can explore for the first time what it really means to be human. This quest will not be restricted to a small minority of seekers or holy men; it will be a pilgrimage by the millions, a search for the billion manifestations of increased human capacity. It will not be easy, this journey into *terra incognita*. Without clear maps, without safe travel instructions, without comforting exhortations, we can only follow delight like a hound on a trail.

We cannot guess what the distant future will ask of its schools, but perhaps we can step far enough into the future to see what our children *already* need. Schools for what?

- To learn the commonly agreed-upon skills and knowledge of the ongoing culture (reading, writing, figuring, history and the like), to learn joyfully and to learn that all of it, even the most sacred "fact," is strictly tentative.
- To learn how to ring creative changes on all that is currently agreed upon.
- To learn delight, not aggression; sharing, not eager acquisition; uniqueness, not narrow competition.
- To learn heightened awareness and control of emotional sensory and bodily states and, through them, increased empathy for other people, perhaps the most common form of ecstasy.
- To learn how to learn, for learning—one word that includes singing, dancing, interacting and much more—is already becoming the main purpose of life.

Such activities may seem to lead far from the school in which your youngster is now enrolled. And yet, in the deepest sense, they spring from the original American impulse toward hope and individual fulfillment. They spring, too, from a personal journey that began in an "ordinary" U.S. public school some 13 years ago.

The fall of 1955 was a difficult time for American teachers. It was two years before the Russian Sputnik was to go up and bring down a deluge of criticism on U.S. schoolmen; but already, a vague discontent was in the air, encouraging a band of critics to launch attacks upon the educational establishment. Almost every national periodical had its own "expert." Most of them followed the basic-education line; that is, they scathingly attacked teachers and "educationists" while offering a curious remedy for all of education's ills: "Go back"—back to the three R's, back to phonics, back to tough, no-nonsense subject-matter drill, back to McGuffey's Readers.

Against this backdrop, I found myself assigned to produce a lengthy magazine feature on what my editor called "the plight of the teacher in America." The assignment offered all the freedom and prerogatives a journalist could wish. There were no preconditions or preconceptions. I could travel anywhere in the country I liked, take as long as I needed, call on any expert for consultation or for authorship of part of the feature.

Expert I was not, never having written a word on the subject of education, never having visited a classroom except as a parent with daughters in the second and third grades. Aware of this lack, I plunged into the assignment, reading as much as I could on the subject, meeting with leading educators and their detractors. I found that my lack of expertise was an advantage. In a year when most education writers carried axes to grind, my naïveté pleased.

The assignment captured me. Dropping any notion of calling in outside help, I went ahead with plans to do all the writing myself. I would depend heavily on a picture story about one teacher. Through the teacher's day-by-day experiences, photographer Charlotte Brooks and I would try to illuminate the matters under debate in a way that would transcend diatribe and expertise. So we set out across the midlands of Illinois, visiting medium-sized schools in medium-sized towns on days when nothing out of the ordinary was happening, seeking one teacher who might, in some respect, represent a million more.

We came into Decatur, Ill., before the end of harvest, and we were still there when the snows were falling. Garfield School was an old, gloomy, blocklike structure of the kind you have seen or imagined a thousand times. Its staff was neither the best nor the worst I had encountered. And the second-grade classroom presided over by a young second-year teacher named Carolyn Wilson was, on the surface, like any number of others. But it was here we decided to stay, to risk our project on the premise that the "ordinary" events in that room were not ordinary at all.

At first, we perceived only a fraction of what was happening. Then we began to realize that 28 children represented 28 little dramas exploding around us at every moment. Perceiving, we were overwhelmed. We were tumbled in a surf of impressions. Charlotte would focus on one situation, and then, before she could click the shutter, something would happen on the periphery of her vision, and she would whirl around to capture a moment already gone. We became obsessed with the lives in that room. After school, we talked of nothing else, endlessly pondering the maze of interaction between children and children, between children and teacher. We learned. Charlotte's camera became more accurate. She was there at the high moments. Still, it was all too swift. The click of the camera lagged a fraction of a second behind the action. We both felt as if we were swimming endlessly against a current.

Gradually, as the weeks passed, we became part of Carolyn Wilson's class. We found ourselves sitting on the floor among the children. They didn't seem to consider it strange. We got onto their verbal level and into their lives. Everything began working. What had been hard became easy. The click of Charlotte's camera made perfect accompaniment to the action, pizzicato accents in a ballet. Carolyn rushed to the lavatory with a boy who was about to vomit. Somehow, Charlotte was there ahead of him, in position, camera focused. And one afternoon just after lunch, she caught an elfin, yellow-haired boy in the very act of learning. It was, I later wrote, one of "those magic moments when knowledge leaps across the gap like a spark, and a child flings up his hand, exulting, 'I know. I *know!*' "

In Carolyn Wilson's class, the educational haggling in the periodicals simply faded into irrelevance. How could anyone smugly prescribe "intellectual rigor" for Sherryl, whose parents had just separated, leaving her half-crippled by anxiety? What did "concentration on subject-matter content" mean to Harold, who sometimes came to school tired and hungry. Charlotte and I were appalled at the teacher's situation. Society had carelessly heaped Herculean tasks upon her— and she just didn't have the tools, the techniques, the environment to do what was required. The solutions offered by the basic-education writers seemed not only inadequate but malicious.

We visited other towns, other classrooms. I looked into educational experiments and investigated the critics' main charges. Something obviously was wrong with the schools, but it was certainly not what the critics were saying. I completed my assignment in a fury of admiration for teachers. They needed more understanding and help, not self-righteous slander.

These feelings were revealed in the feature, *What Is a Teacher?*, and included pictures, text and "A Magna Carta for Teachers." By the time it came out in LOOK (February 21, 1956), I was at work on something else and never dreamed of doing more stories on education. But *What Is a Teacher?* would not release me so easily. It struck some sort of chord and quickly stirred up the familiar concomitants of "success"—showers of letters, requests for reprints, awards, translation into many languages. So, I often found myself in school again in the years that followed, reporting on gifted children, school boards, superintendents, slum schools, vocational education, testing, programmed instruction and the like. I worked hard at not becoming an expert. I tried to approach each story as if it were my first.

But I moved away from *What Is a Teacher?* I became increasingly concerned not with the way things are but how they could be. New experiments showed how we had underrated children's ability to learn. New techniques to help children learn—just what teachers needed, it seemed to me—became available. And I became involved with education outside of journalism.

I guess it was inevitable I would fall out of love with that first story. There is a modern disease of detachment and despair that has infected many of our most noted intellectuals; the symptoms include a morbid fear of enthusiasm and an inability to perceive hope in any situation. The disease is highly contagious. I was not immune. *What Is a Teacher?*—enthusiastic, hopeful, emotional—began to seem embarrassingly naïve and starry-eyed to me. I found myself omitting it when people asked for reprints of my past education stories. I wanted to be as full of existential despair as the next writer.

That was some years ago. I hope I have been cured. A certain naïveté is prerequisite to all learning. A certain optimism is prerequisite to all action. When a nation's best minds desert all hope and decry all enthusiasm, they leave the nation susceptible to nihilism and anarchy. When they refuse to be committed, they leave commitment to those who would destroy, not build; those who would go back, not forward. Existential despair is the ultimate cop-out. I'll have no more of it.

And now I leaf through a copy of *What Is a Teacher?* Thirteen years is archaeological time in the field of magazines. One of the pages is torn. The pictures seem faded. But the moments are vivid, and the thesis seems right. I do not deny my enthusiasm. A yellow-haired boy flings up his hand. A tearful boy with a crew cut pulls away from Carolyn Wilson's embrace, resisting forgiveness. A doleful little girl nestles in the curve of Carolyn's body. And, on page after page, the teacher is there, struggling cheerfully against impossible odds, bolstered by unsubstantiated hope, saying, "There is good in every child."

I reach for the future from Carolyn Wilson's classroom (though there will be no classrooms). I borrow my spirit of hope from her and the hundreds of teachers I have known (though there will be no teachers as we now think of them). And if my school of the future seems a radical departure, it is only because the human potential I have found in schools like Garfield in Decatur, Ill., demands we now take radical measures.

SOCIAL ENVIRONMENT

From the White House Conference on Children (Forum 19)

The children of America are the future of America, yet they are now far from being the nation's first priority. Both public policies and programs and our actions as individuals shape a world in many ways inhospitable, indeed often hostile, to the life of children and their full creative growth.

The United States is a new phenomenon in human history, a society with the technical capacity to feed, house, and clothe all its members comfortably and to create an environment that is good for all its children. Our failure to create the humane world within our reach is not the result of irresistible forces of nature working against us; it is our own attitudes and actions that have made our living envi-

"Social Environment." From *Report to the President: White House Conference on Children* (Washington, D.C., U.S. Government Printing Office, 1970).

ronment less than the liberating framework for human joy and creation that it could be.

But our concerns have been elsewhere. And before such an environment will emerge, fundamental changes are essential—in attitudes, in policies, and in programs.

We tend to compartmentalize our world, separating the worlds of the young and the old, the urban and the rural, the ghetto-dweller and the suburbanite; the problems seem more manageable when they are considered in discrete pieces.

Our transportation system is a case in point. The day may come when we develop a coherent, humane, national environment because our children cannot play outdoors without choking on polluted air. Or such a policy may come because adults cannot travel to and from central cities without insufferable delays.

Our transportation abuses our environment in ways that compromise the quality of life for both children and adults. Nearly half the air pollution that afflicts the playgrounds of our children would be eliminated by the exclusion of automobiles moving into and out of our cities. Efficient, coordinated transit systems could also minimize delays and free urban man from today's costly dependence on the automobile.

It is foolish to consider these problems as separate ones; the problems we create in our environment for our children generally have the same roots as problems of adults; the world of children and the world of adults are the same.

We also have a habit of separating physical problems from social problems in our thinking. Those most interested in the physical environment focus their attention on air and water pollution, noise, the preservation of open spaces, or the visual abominations afflicting our surroundings. Those who champion social concerns think about segregation, substandard housing, poverty, or juvenile delinquency.

Yet these are not two separate classes of problems. The physical environment influences the social environment; the social environment often determines how we deal with the physical environment.

Those more interested in social problems will try to change traffic patterns in the hope of diminishing the number of children killed each year on our streets and highways, in the hope of eliminating highways which slice through both low and high income neighborhoods, and in the hope of modifying the pattern of living whereby the affluent draw their income in the city but live and pay taxes in the suburbs.

For those who would plan environmental improvement, an important part of the job is to fit together the pieces which we usually attempt to handle separately. No single, coherent policy yet exists to serve as an organizing principle for the problems described briefly in the next few pages.

Consider air pollution. Probably more than any other physical disequilibrium, air pollution is apparent to Americans as a serious problem. Each of us contributes to it by his way of life: we drive cars when we could use buses or trains; we permit buses with dirty engines to idle for long periods; we burn fuels for heat. In a negative sense we contribute to air pollution by not demanding that commercial and industrial abusers of the environment mend their ways. Ecologists are quick to point out that the enemy of the physical environment is each one of us acting heedlessly. In the cartoons, Pogo put it beautifully, "We have met the enemy and they is us."

But our social environment suffers as well; air pollution, like other problems which appear to be exclusively physical, has its social repercussions. More concentrated in some localities than others, it makes certain areas more or less desirable as places to live and work. Those who cannot move away are thus segregated from those who can. And such social separation generally speeds economic deterioration; older shopping areas decline and tax bases slip. The residents of a dirty mill town can suffer a loss of worth as well in the eyes of others and in their own. The heaviest penalty for our way of life falls on the old, the young, the sick, and the poor.

Consider water pollution. The rivers passing through many of our major cities are open sewers; a number of our rivers and lakes will no longer support even normal aquatic life. As human population near the oceans increases, and as we expand our use of oceans for transportation and other purposes, even these bodies of water are being measurably polluted. Thor Heyerdahl, in his recent journey across the Atlantic, reported that for days at a time he could not get a bucket of water from the open sea which was not polluted with congealed oil.

Consider noise pollution. Noise levels increase as populations grow more concentrated. People themselves do not make most of the noise; it is made by the devices used to support our technologically advanced way of life. In metropolitan areas the sound of trucks, cars, airplanes, pneumatic hammers, and even power mowers are all but impossible to avoid. During working hours in downtown New York City, it is difficult and irritating to engage in normal conversation. Even in the protected environment of the home, we are exposed to the almost incessant noise of television, washing machines, air conditioners, amplified music, and dishwashers. . . .

Consider transportation. Since World War II, in a period of accelerated urban migration and suburban development, our public transit services have actually declined. The major transportation load is still within cities, rather than between cities and suburbs. Yet nearly all major urban transportation investment has been devoted to the needs of the minority—to freeways serving automobile traffic to and from the suburbs. Mass transit has been permitted to decay.

The major impetus to this pattern has been the abundance of Federal funds for expressways, and the consequent scarcity of funds for other means of transportation, including both mass transit and the improvement of major arterial streets.

Suburban car ownership has reached the point where two cars (or more) are considered by millions as an absolute necessity. Those who have no cars must suffer the consequence of highly restricted mobility.

Who are these have-nots? They are the handicapped, the poor, the elderly—and the young. The subsidized school bus does not meet the need for cheap transportation after school hours to the library, the museum, the zoo, or the park. Our transportation policies deny many of our young people access to the world of experience.

Clearly, one thing needed is a participative process of metropolitan transportation planning—right down to the neighborhood and block level—oriented toward increasing the mobility of those whose needs have been pushed aside by our present transportation policies and programs.

The Wall Street Journal, Wednesday, December 2, 1970
By Richard Stone, *Staff Reporter of The Wall Street Journal*

NEW YORK—On a dark night six months ago, a shadowy figure stood before a dilapidated, abandoned apartment building on Manhattan's Upper West Side. Lifting a crowbar, he wrenched loose the sheet metal nailed over the door of the dingy building. Then he ushered his wife and their five children inside.

That's how Jose Rivera found a home.

Today the Riveras are still living in the building they seized from the city's Housing and Development Administration—a building the city had slated for destruction to clear the way for an urban renewal project. Though the city has taken no action yet—and, in fact, is supplying utilities—it seems almost certain that eventually the Riveras, along with over 150 other families who have become urban squatters in recent months, will be forced to vacate the building they seized with "the law of the crowbar."

Replacing a Corpse

Others try to keep track of obituaries to divine what deaths are creating rent-control vacancies. A New York public relations man who lives in a rent-controlled apartment building recently learned of the death of a neighbor living in a bigger apartment. "I was on the phone to the landlord within two hours after that lady died," he says, "and I was too late. Someone else had already taken her place."

Another New Yorker recently happened to see two policemen wheeling a shrouded corpse from a rent-controlled apartment building. He hurried into the lobby to find the superintendent. "That's a shame to see someone die like that," he commiserated, barely concealing his eagerness.

"She was 92," snapped the super. "It was her time to go."

"Still, it's too bad," countered the man. "But I suppose that does leave a vacancy, doesn't it?"

"Nope," grinned the super. "She was my mother-in-law. I've got the apartment now."

Consider housing. The President's Committee on Urban Housing calculated that the nation would have to provide, over ten years, 26 million new and rehabilitated housing units, including at least six million subsidized units for lower income families. Despite the adoption of that figure as a national goal by the Housing Act of 1968, we are not even close to making good on our commitment. Our current monetary policies make it impossible for the private sector to measure up to its technical capacity and Congress has failed to provide the funds needed for subsidies.

Our present housing generally fails to provide each individual in our nation access to privacy, solitude, and silence. Many of our citizens do not have the opportunity to live in homes which are part of an integrated neighborhood. Housing projects are built without full citizen participation and planning, and without access to parks and open spaces. Our housing codes are not standardized, and not universally enforced.

Is the ideal of adequate housing for every American citizen a realistic possibility? Julie Raisch, a young member of this Forum from Minneapolis, Minnesota, submitted the following statements:

> I second the motion on Housing—100%. I think such a housing project is possible. Such a project *does* exist, for I have lived in one. The housing itself is in units: 2-story units joined next to each other, but each individual unit has the wholeness of "I" separate home. An upstairs—bedrooms—2 to 4 bedrooms; a living-room; kitchens; both spacious enough for comfortability; and a full basement (not required if in other parts of the nation), plus area front and back large enough for a child to play on, but *sodded*. The playgrounds were covered by *both* sod and blacktop. The project had Community Involvement and yet asked for more. Programs were Head Start and a nursery school, both well supervised. Projects such as night school (and baby-sitters provided for such nights), lessons in music, and swimming were going on when I lived there. The Community Center would charter a bus for all who attended, to and from the nearby swimming pool. There was volunteer work going on also, such as helping in the co-op or the Child Care Center, minding children on playgrounds, and most impressive—a newspaper for the project tenants only. Plus cats, dogs, and other pets were also permitted, if the pet did not interfere in the welfare and well-being of the other tenants in the projects.
>
> Such a project is possible, for I have lived in one.

Considered the class- and race-segregated pattern of urban growth. Polarization between inner city and suburbs has been encouraged by many government policies and public practices, such as local exclusionary zoning practices; reliance on local, real property taxation as the financial basis for schools and other services; programs for highway building; and Federal mortgage insurance programs. We now see a pattern of urban life which encourages and permits wealthy suburban communities to "zone out" families who cannot pay their way in terms of local property taxes. One ugly consequence in some communities has been restrictions against families with children in order to avoid the need for educational services. Another consequence is *de facto* segregation in schools, and general and damaging separation of children of different races or economic classes. Another is denial of freedom of choice to those families, and their children, who wish to move out of the central city but who cannot because of exclusionary zoning practices. Still another consequence is denial of the basic principle of equal educational opportunity to all children, since the local tax bases of different communities produce school systems of widely varying quality. The present local tax system compounds problems by forcing communities with large numbers of low-income families to provide services from a restricted tax base. As a result of this regressive characteristic, families on stable or declining incomes are often suspicious of any proposal for government spending, even to benefit their own community.

Consider the family and the school. These two elements of the environment either provide, or deprive, the child of opportunities to fulfill some of his most vital needs: physical well-being, a positive self-image, and adequate coping skills for dealing with a world of constant change.

But our families are often fragmented. Children grow up in all but total ignorance of the needs and life patterns of adults. Adults are often unable or unwilling to listen to and understand their children. Schools, too, fail to provide what children need, beyond certain cognitive skills and training for employment. While volumes have been written on what is right and what is wrong with our school systems, a central problem is that education falls very short of being a top national priority.

Consider finally the ways in which we use our land, and the fact that we as a nation have no guiding policy, nor even a guiding philosophy, for how land should be used.

We are recklessly squandering our children's heritage—the natural environment. Our fragmented government agencies, as presently constituted, seem incapable of controlling urban sprawl or the damage and depletion of the natural world by special interests. Ecological boundaries are not necessarily political boundaries. Neither air nor water, which are profoundly affected by the use of land, is limited to geographic or political boundaries. Municipal and county laws and regulations are thus futile until this high degree of ecological interdependence is recognized, and political adjustments are made allowing for a uniform land use policy.

The children of America must become the nation's first priority. Our public policies and programs must be changed to favor an environment for children and adults which is socially humane and physically healthy, one which provides children and their parents with the resources and the richness of experience needed for growth. This reordering of policies and programs will require not only commitment, but massive funding. This Forum believes the funds should come in large part from redistribution of monies now poured into programs which deserve far lower priorities, such as the war in Indochina and the malignant defense complex which nourishes it, and from such wasteful and dangerous projects as the SST and the ABM. The need for money is important, but the need for more humanity on the part of all Americans is vital.

Specifically, the goals of this Forum are:

- A National Land Use policy which will direct our efforts to preserve and improve the environment, both physical and social, in which children grow and develop
- Coordination of the activities of all agencies, public and private, toward achieving a healthy environment for children
- A means to stimulate action at the local level toward bringing the recommendations of this White House Conference into reality, and implementing whatever legislation may result from the recommendations.

This Forum makes three primary recommendations:

- That a National Land Use policy, encompassing both social and physical environments, be developed and implemented
- That all agencies, public and private, recognize the need to communicate, cooperate, and coordinate their activities to achieve a healthy environment in the interest of children
- That a mobilization committee, composed of delegates to this White House Conference, both youth and adults, coordinate and channel citizen community action to implement the many excellent recommendations of this Conference.

Other recommendations, no less important, dealing with specific aspects of problems are grouped under these three primary recommendations.

This Forum recommends that a National Land Use policy, encompassing both social and physical environments, be developed and implemented.

This Forum believes that a National Land Use policy can and should become the instrument under which the various environmental problems can be brought into their proper relationships. In general, a National Land Use policy would guide us in determining the uses to which we put different portions of our land, and our distribution over the land of the human population with its various activities of living and working. It would include provision for consideration of population densities; for planning communities of optimum size; for protection of land, water, and air from pollution and overuse; for housing; for institutions, including schools; for transportation requirements, both in terms of the distribution of activities which require transportation, and of land devoted to transportation facilities; for community zoning; and for the taxation practices which both underlie zoning restrictions and pay for community services.

No policy can solve all our problems at a stroke. But a sound policy can help us to see where our best interests lie, both nationally and locally, and can help us to work together instead of pulling against each other. A National Land Use policy thus can provide the matrix within which we may analyze our many environmental problems and their relationships, and begin to move toward solutions.

We recommend that a strong commission on environmental control be developed at the national level.

We recommend that city and county governments be consolidated into area-wide governments, with size and boundaries appropriate to natural ecological divisions, and with the power to interpret and apply land use policies throughout the area.

We recommend that each such government develop and establish a Community Development program. Such programs are required as the local blueprints—in effect, the local land use policies—for renovating the physical and social environment. A broad variety of professions should be involved in formulating the programs: until now, financial, political, and architectural leaders have dominated city planning efforts. Ecologists must now take their place in the planning, and planners must be educated about man and his environment.

An adequate Community Development program must include:

- Community planning, leadership, and decision making. Since the people in the community are best acquainted with their own structure, they must exercise self-determination. The program should be developed by representatives of all segments of society, including representation from inner cities, suburbs, rural areas, Indian communities, and migrant communities.
- Community Service Centers. The residents of the development area must have knowledge of and access to all social, medical, recreational, economic, and cultural services and resources.
- Pollution control. The survival and welfare of our children and ourselves demand effective control of pollution. Probably the greatest public health problems in the future will be not the control of specific diseases, but the control of pollution of the general environment. Until now, we have been concerned mainly with treating the symptoms of ecological imbalances; we must now concern ourselves with eliminating the causes.
- Recreation. Recreation plays an indispensable part in the physical and social development of children.
- Transportation. Without adequate, low-cost transportation, the social, cultural, and educational resources of the community will be denied to children and adults.
- Security. A healthy community needs safety through equitable law enforcement, preferably by community residents.
- Population level. Each community, faced with its own set of environmental limitations, needs to attempt to determine its own optimal population. Obviously, food is not the only limiting factor, since many communities will be able to feed far more "warm bodies" than can live there as human beings developing to the limits of their own potential. Therefore, each community should begin to probe the question of the optimum population level for its own conditions.
- Racial and economic integration. Only by living, working, and

playing together can we begin to understand and accept each other. Adults furnish the models for the development of children. We cannot hope to see our children escape the restrictive effects of segregation unless we begin to furnish appropriate models.

- Rehabilitation of facilities. Adequate present facilities should not be destroyed merely to build new ones. Unnecessary destruction is not only uneconomic, but in the case of historical structures, tends to weaken our sense of continuity with the past.

- Access to places of work. Work locations and access to them should be planned to ensure that each person has available the widest possible variety of jobs, and therefore the greatest opportunity to apply and develop his talents.

- Zoning on ecological principles. Zoning regulations should be determined by the nature of the land and by boundaries based on ecological differences, rather than by political convenience. Zoning should strictly control industries that are, or might become, gross polluters.

- Funding. Funds for community development should be solicited from all sources, public and private. However, no funds should be made available to any community project unless the project conforms to the principles established here.

We recommend on all levels efforts be made to get more land into public ownership, and that "open space" bills be introduced which will enable private owners to establish scenic easements and other restrictions on the use of land.

We recommend that metropolitan and area governments explore the possibilities and problems of making available new lands for development in accordance with sound ecological practices.

We recommend that new communities be established outside major metropolitan areas to enable people to live in moderate-sized cities with access to unspoiled countryside.

We recommend that governments encourage the development of industries in rural areas, when ecological considerations permit, thus providing occupations and cultural opportunities more nearly equal to those found in cities.

We recommend that adequate housing programs be planned

and funded to meet the basic needs of children: privacy, comfort, a broad variety of experiences, and a safe environment in which to work and play. This Forum is unequivocably committed to the ideal of adequate housing for every American.

The following are required to realize this ideal:

• Congress should provide at least the funding necessary to reach the national goal, established in the Housing Act of 1968, of 26 million new and rehabilitated units, including at least 6 million subsidized units for low income families, within ten years of the date of the Act.

• Our national monetary policies should be modified to permit and encourage the private sector to perform up to its technical capacity to meet the housing demand.

• Government regulatory bodies should establish national health and sanitation standards, and adopt measures to ensure compliance.

• The housing industry and government regulatory bodies should work toward standardized housing codes with provision for penalties severe enough to ensure compliance.

• State and local code bodies should review and modify their building codes to permit materials and practices which tend to reduce costs and speed construction, while maintaining performance standards, and to establish orderly procedures to expedite testing and adoption of future improvements.

• The housing industry and the building trades should support the use and further development of new materials and practices that tend to lower costs and speed construction, while maintaining performance standards.

• All planning for community development should include full citizen participation.

In all development or renewal plans: provision should be made to encourage a representative mix of income levels and races; provision should be made for social services, such as comprehensive child care programs; full attention should be given to aesthetic and cultural values of both new and old neighborhoods, and new housing should be architecturally and environmentally compatible with the best qualities of the surrounding neighborhoods; and provision should be made for museums, performing arts centers, outdoor sculpture, and other facilities for art and culture, easily accessible to highly populated areas.

We recommend that transportation patterns and programs in metropolitan areas be reordered to reflect the physical and social needs of the community. High speed mass transportation systems, responsive to the needs of the community, should supplant the private automobile as the main means of transportation.

Public funding for transportation should be heavily concentrated in mass transit systems, including buses and above- and underground rail systems. Local transportation authorities should be encouraged and helped to design and operate local rapid transit systems.

All expressways between the city and its environs should have one lane designated for bus traffic only, to improve bus service to the inner city and encourage its use.

The use of private automobiles should be sharply curtailed or prohibited in the business districts of cities.

Wherever possible, streets should be reconverted to open space, planted as parks or gardens, or made available for recreation.

All planning decisions should be made with full participation of local citizen groups.

We recommend that all agencies, public and private, recognize the need to communicate, cooperate, and coordinate their activities to achieve a healthy environment in the interest of children.

Programs must be developed through inter-agency planning, and must include a system of accountability which will result in better service to children and youth. Since services are effective at the local level, this Forum anticipates the failure of all its major recommendations unless communities develop inter-agency cooperation. Therefore, we further urge:

- That government at all levels identify all agencies concerned with children and the environment
- That governments set up mechanisms for inter-agency coordination
- That governments stimulate interdisciplinary training for all persons involved in these agencies

- That appropriation committees at all levels adopt a policy of refusing to fund any agency or program which does not provide for appropriate inter-agency action.

We recommend that a Mobilization Committee, composed of delegates to this White House Conference, both youth and adults, coordinate and channel citizen community action to implement the many excellent recommendations of this Conference.

In the White House Conference process, members of all Forums have met and conferred under the aegis of the national government, with the purpose of proposing and influencing the passage of legislation toward certain defined goals. While acknowledging the strengths of this process, we conclude that no legislation, however commendable, can be an effective instrument of social change unless some structure exists to coordinate action at the local level.

We urge that the members of this present White House Conference on Children undertake the responsibility of stimulating and coordinating such action.

Recent history indicates that the impact of youth on our society has on the whole been one of conscience and sober responsibility. Yet young Americans, striving to act as good citizens, find few positions of responsibility open to them. We believe that a new thrust is imperative. One workable answer is to mobilize a force of youth and concerned adults that will inform and stimulate local action, not to start a host of new organizations, but to act on and through present local groups and agencies.

Therefore we urge:

- That a power base be constructed to serve as a focal point for the concerns of our youth, and from which government officials at all levels can be approached for their cooperation
- That delegates to this Conference commit themselves to extending the White House Conference process through mobilization and organization within their own communities
- That a central Mobilization Committee be constituted, composed of three members of each of the state delegations to this Conference; and that of the three, at least one must be youth and at least one must represent a minority group

- That this Committee be completely autonomous
- That this Committee seek widespread sanction, endorsement, and funding, but without in any way or degree compromising its autonomy
- That Conference delegates act as a primary link between the Mobilization Committee and local communities.

We further urge that both the Mobilization Committee and the individual delegates maintain a close rapport with the progress of the White House Conference process; that they extend that rapport as far as possible to communities and local groups; and that they work through responsible local groups, agencies, and programs to coordinate and stimulate action to implement the results of the White House Conference process.